More!
Phonics Through Poetry

Teaching Phoenemic Awareness Using Poetry

Babs Bell Hajdusiewicz

Illustrated by

Daniel L. Grant

Good Year Books

are available for most basic curriculum subjects plus many enrichment areas. For more Good Year Books, contact your local bookseller or educational dealer. For a complete catalog with information about other Good Year Books, please write:

Good Year Books
1900 East Lake Avenue
Glenview, IL 60025

Cover: *Poem:* "Conversations" by Ellen Raieta. Copyright © 1997 by Ellen Raieta. Reprinted by permission of the author. *Illustration:* Lindy Burnett.

Book Design: Lynne Grenier.

Acquisitions Manager: Bobbie Dempsey.

Production/Manufacturing Director: Janet Yearian.

Production/Manufacturing Coordinator: Roxanne Knoll.

Focusing Talk™ is a trademark of Babs Bell Hajdusiewicz.
ISBN 0-673-36346-5

5 6 7 8 9 – ML – 06 05 04 03 02 01

This Book Is Printed
On Recycled Paper

Contents

ch as in **chin**

Final Blends

Introduction

A child's name is one of the first words that she tries to read or write. And the first letter of her name is often first letter name she learns. Why is this? Because her name is familiar! She's heard it thousands of times. She's said it over and over. Her name is a word that has meaning and purpose. She's ready and *eager* to meet that word in print!

One of our most important goals as teachers, parents, and caregivers of young children is to prepare them for success as readers and writers. Research and experience tell us that children are most likely to be successful in reading and writing a word if they've had repeated experiences with hearing and saying the individual sounds in the word. Studies have also shown that an effective activity to train children's ears and tongues involves repeated readings of literature selections that "play" with language sounds.

The rhythm and rhyme of poetry make it ideally suited to providing repeated experiences with the individual sounds of language. The brevity of words, rhythmic language, and frequently occurring rhyming patterns encourage ears to listen and tongues to repeat the sounds and words. Additionally, poems tell stories or introduce ideas in ways that are meaningful to young listeners. And poems very often invite children to reflect . . . and to laugh!

The playful language of children's poems is best enjoyed when poems are read aloud. Reading poems aloud presents valuable opportunities for children to hear the sounds of language. Focusing Talk™ around the words and ideas from familiar poems during everyday conversation encourages children to try out those familiar sounds and words on their own tongues. Practice with hearing and saying words and breaking them into their individual sounds provides children with a wealth of oral language experiences. Children who are equipped with oral language skills are prepared for success in phonics instruction—ready to meet letters and associate those letters with familiar and meaningful sounds—prepared and *eager* to enjoy success as readers and writers.

More Phonics Through Poetry: Teaching Phonemic Awareness Using Poetry is a read-aloud collection of poems, activities, and accompanying information to help you prepare children for success in reading and writing through repeated experiences with the sounds of language.

The purpose of this book is to provide teachers, parents, and caregivers with two or more meaningful, interesting, and enticing poems that target each of the following sounds of language: consonant digraphs, final blends, 3-letter blends, diphthongs, word endings, other vowel sounds (*u* as in *full*, schwa *a* as in *mama*, etc.), plural forms, possessives, *r*-controlled vowels and vowel digraphs, prefixes and suffixes, and contractions; in addition, two final poems focus on letters that are silent in some words. Each poem is meant to be read aloud so that children hear a particular language sound again and again in word after word, all within a meaningful context.

Accompanying each poem are word lists grouped according to phonics sounds found in the poem, activity ideas that involve children in the use of phonics sounds, and other suggestions to assist you in presenting the poem and its targeted sound. Included are ways to extend the poem through Focusing Talk around its words and ideas during conversations and interactions, illustrating for children how they can use these same sounds and words when *they* talk and interact with others. The Focusing Talk ideas for using figurative language are especially helpful for children who are learning English as a second language.

More general suggestions for reading aloud, Focusing Talk, and finding time for poetry and sound-awareness training in your busy days with children appear in the section entitled "Building Awareness of Sounds." The phonics activities that complete that section and the blackline masters (at the back of the book) for making letter cards provide additional tools for initiating phonics instruction, introducing children to the letters that represent familiar sounds. Finally, various indexes offer ready access to all the poems and sounds in the book.

How to Use This Book

This collection, one of a two-book series, contains 112 illustrated poems that are intended to be read aloud to young children. Each poem in the collection focuses on an individual language sound, one that may be spelled in a variety of ways. In each poem, a targeted sound is heard repeatedly, providing many examples of that language sound in word after word after word. While some poems in the collection will twist your tongue, others will provide fun and learning in a variety of other ways. Yet, in every poem (except, of course, those targeting silent letters), you will hear a sound repeated again and again.

This book is designed so that the poems and sounds may be presented in any sequence that suits your individual needs. To assist you in locating the poems that emphasize a particular sound, the poems are organized as follows:

Consonant Digraphs

Final Blends

3-letter Blends

Diphthongs

Word Endings

Other Vowel Sounds

Plurals and Possessives

R-controlled Vowels and Vowel Digraphs

Prefixes and Suffixes

Contractions

Silent Letters

You will find two or three poems that target each sound. In addition, most of the poems in this book feature more repetitive sounds than the one being targeted. Thus for any given sound, you may wish to draw on some of these other poems. The index of sounds at the back of the book will help you locate all of the poems for a particular sound.

For ease in presenting some similar sounds, such as *s*/soft *c* as in *so/city,* plural *-s/-es/-ies* as in *dogs/buses/babies,* and possessive *'s* as in *dad's,* you will find these sounds targeted separately. Note that poems targeting sounds other than those covered in this book (long vowels, short vowels, consonants, initial blends) can be found in its companion, *Phonics Through Poetry: Teaching Phonemic Awareness Using Poetry.*

Each poem is accompanied by helpful information designed to assist you in using the poem to build children's oral language skills and develop their awareness of the individual sounds of language. Look for the following categories to help you present each poem and its targeted sound:

Targeted Sound

Additional Sound(s)

Focusing Talk

Activity

Listen! Listen! Hear That Sound?

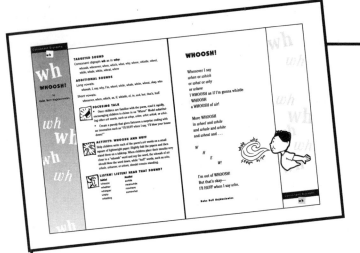

Targeted Sound

This section notes the sound that is heard repeatedly in the accompanying poem. Along with its phonetic term and a sample word, the targeted sound is followed by a list of words in the poem that include that sound. This list of words will be helpful as you use the poem to build a child's awareness of sounds within words. Later, when children are associating sounds with their corresponding letter names, the list of words will be a valuable aid in focusing attention on different spellings of the same sound.

A poem that targets the sound of -nk (as in pink) will include many words, or repetitions of words, that contain the sound of -nk as in pink. The poem may also include words in which n or k appears; however, these words will not be listed in the sections. Note that poems targeting the individual consonant sounds can be found in the first book of this series, Phonics Through Poetry: Teaching Phonemic Awareness Using Poetry.

Additional Sound(s)

Some poems offer good examples of sounds other than those being targeted. Look here for each additional sound along with its phonetic term, a sample word, and a list of the poem's words that include the sound. In some cases,

you'll find sounds collected under their group names. For instance, a poem containing many words with different consonant digraphs will have those words listed under a "Consonant Digraphs" category. Use this listing to review the sounds of various consonant digraphs or to help children differentiate among the sounds.

Focusing Talk™

This is where you will find some practical and easy suggestions for modeling the use of the poem's vocabulary and ideas in your daily conversations and interactions with children. Many of the suggestions focus on ways to present poem-related figurative language. Such experiences are especially helpful for children who are learning English as a second language. Other suggestions provide meaningful ways to converse with children using new words or expressions that include the targeted sound. As you and the children "live" with a poem's words and content, you'll want to jot down in the margins your own ideas for Focusing Talk around the poem. For additional discussion of focusing talk, consult the section that follows entitled Building Awareness of Sounds.

Activity

Look here for a poem-related activity that involves children in practical use of the poem's language and ideas. You'll find that many of the activity ideas are well-suited for use in your learning centers.

Listen! Listen! Hear That Sound?

This final section features lists of words, other than those in the poem, that include the targeted sound. Each word list is organized according to the targeted sound's position in a word—initial, medial, or final. The lists are intended as resources for additional experiences with the targeted sound. For example, you may decide to focus on some of the words during conversations with children, include the words in activities within themes and lessons, or incorporate the words into the various Phonics Link activity suggestions beginning on page 10 of this book. You'll want to add other words here that include the targeted sound, as you and the children meet those words in conversation or in print.

Blackline Masters

The blackline masters beginning on page 257 can be reproduced to make letter cards that correspond to the targeted sounds in this book. Copy the blackline masters onto heavy paper or cardstock, laminate, and cut on the dotted lines to provide letter cards for each child.

Indexes

Various indexes at the back of the book help you locate any one of the poems, or sounds provided. You will find all poems indexed by Title, Author, First Line, Sound, and Theme.

Building Awareness of Sounds

Reading Aloud

Reading aloud "spreads a buffet" of oral vocabulary and knowledge that fill children's "pockets" with words and ideas for use in their daily living. Many teachers, parents, and caregivers set aside at least one period each day to read aloud to children. Reading aloud prepares children for success in reading and writing, as it models how words on a printed page can be spoken. Reading aloud also prepares children to meet print, as it models how individual sounds fit together to make words, and how those words fit together in phrases and sentences to suggest meaningful ideas. And very importantly, reading aloud shares the joy of reading!

It is helpful to read a new poem aloud at least twice. Repetition gives children the opportunity to focus on particular sounds, words, or ideas that are especially meaningful or interesting. Rereading a new poem also lets children begin to predict words in order to share in the reading—making those sounds, words, and ideas their own! Indeed, a shared reading experience is a natural outcome when we read aloud. Children are eager to join in on repeated readings, confident that they can complete a rhyming line or recall a familiar passage.

We know from experience that children like to repeat interesting words and ideas and that children tend to repeat those words exactly as they hear them. Thus, you'll want to introduce new poems with expression and enthusiasm, such that children can "feel" each sound, word, phrase, and sentence.

You may want to recite "The Index," a useful poetic tool that keeps children's attention focused as you're using the index to find a particular poem:

> If I don't know
>
> On which page to look,
>
> I'll use the index
>
> In the back of my book.

Children will not only listen to the words—they will begin to use those words, themselves, to locate print in books!

Each time you read a poem aloud, consider employing a simple introductory routine that helps children associate an author's name with a poem. For example, if you say, "'When It Comes to Bugs' by Aileen Fisher. Thank you, Aileen Fisher," before sharing the poem, children see that a person, just like themselves, has written and shared the words they are about to enjoy. This introductory routine also encourages children to talk and write in order to share their own thoughts—*and* to feel confident that their contributions will be appreciated, too!

Focusing Talk

Reading aloud to children presents a "buffet" of language and knowledge that is full of all sorts of "tasty" words and ideas. One of the best ways to help children "taste" those morsels and then put them in their "pockets" is to use the language of familiar read-alouds, such as the poems in this collection, as you converse and interact with children. When children hear the words and ideas from a familiar read-aloud used in meaningful ways again and again, the sounds in the words become so familiar that children want to try out the words on their own tongues, and use that language when *they* talk and interact with others.

Focusing Talk is a natural and easy way to engage children, while building oral language experiences. Focusing Talk around familiar literature bridges "book talk" and "talk talk," as it models for children how printed sounds and words can be used in other meaningful contexts. Modeled use of the language of literature illustrates for children how individual sounds fit together to make words, and how words combine to make phrases and sentences that have meaning. Modeled use of such language also shows children how words, and sometimes their meanings, change when endings, prefixes, or suffixes are added. Further, Focusing Talk models meaningful use of figurative language, an especially helpful experience for children who are learning English as a second language.

Focusing Talk around a familiar piece of literature, such as a poem, allows you to "read aloud" anywhere, any time. When conversation recalls a familiar poem, the effect is as though the selection, itself, has just been read aloud again. That valuable bridging of "book talk" and "talk talk" occurs every time conversation includes *quoted lines or entire passages* from printed materials. Likewise, children experience the close relationship between oral language and written language when *innovations on the book language* personalize its words, or *references to the literature* call the selection's

words and ideas to mind in a general way or through the use of similes and metaphors.

Focusing Talk models for children the very purpose of all reading—to take words right off the printed page and personalize them for use in everyday talking. Think about how that might happen in the following examples, in which talk is focused around the well-known favorite "Twinkle Twinkle":

■ Quoting the Text

Quote a word, a phrase, a line, or the entire poem (or, in this case, sing it) to comment on a real or pictured star or nighttime sky. You might also say, "Twinkle, twinkle, little star!" to compliment a child's excellent performance, or sing, "How I wonder what you are!" to a costumed child.

■ Innovating on the Text

Change the poem's words as appropriate to comment on a particular situation or experience. For example, you might say, "Twinkle twinkle, big brown eyes," to a child whose eyes are aglow with excitement or mirth. Similarly, you might say, "How I wonder where you are!" as you're searching for a lost item or when a child is playing hide-and-seek.

■ Referring to the Text

Refer to the poem to associate its words or ideas with a real or pictured star in a nighttime sky. You might make a general reference to the poem this way: "There's a twinkling star high in the sky," or "I see a diamond that's twinkling." Using a metaphor or simile based on the poem, you might describe a child as a "shining star" or say, "Your whole face is twinkling like a sky full of stars!"

Finding Time

So how do you find time in your already-full day to build children's awareness of sounds through the use of poetry? It's easy, when you consider the goals of your curriculum, your daily routines, *and* the time that you and children spend conversing and interacting throughout the day. Here are some ways to incorporate poetry and sound-awareness training into your busy days with children—*without* stealing time from other activities:

- Dedicate one of your read-aloud periods each week to the introduction and enjoyment of poems that provide sound-awareness training. Share two or three new poems during the period. Then begin the next week's read-aloud period with those now-familiar poems, before introducing two or three new poems. The repetition each week will help your children put the language of those poems in their "pockets." And as weeks go by, children's personal repertoires of learned sounds, words, and ideas will grow . . . and grow . . . and grow!

- Introduce poems from this collection when you are focusing on particular sounds. Children will enjoy meeting "Chipmunkskunkdonkmonkey," "Skink and Skunk," or "Hummingbird" when they are learning about the sound of final blend *-nk*. Let "Bird Alert" or "Thirty Dirty Turtles" add interest to your lessons on the sound of *r*-controlled vowel *ur*. The index of sounds at the back of this book will help you locate poems for any given sound.

- Introduce a poem within a theme or lesson in any aspect of your curriculum. A study of seasons might include "Ode to Spring," "A Walk in Fall," "In Springtime," or "Four Seasons." Add interesting language and ideas to a families theme with "Brother," "What Clarissa Likes," "A Walk in Fall," or "Tearful Night Noises." Share "Joyful Finish," "Too Blunt," or "I Did It!" when focusing on manners, values, or self-esteem issues. The index of themes at the back of this book will help you locate poems you can incorporate into your every theme and lesson.

- Begin or end each day with a poem. You may want to invite children to help select a "Poem of the Week." Reread the poem each morning or afternoon during the week, and you'll hear children eagerly joining in to say the words with you—and soon, all by themselves!

- Introduce a poem to describe how you feel or how a child appears to be feeling. Share thoughts or observations with "Posing," "The Thinker," "Following Rules at School," or "It's a Puzzle!"

- Use a poem to aid in classroom management—that is, do your nagging poetically! Read "Too Blunt," "Disorder," or "Bulldog Bully" to serve as a meaningful and gentle reminder about a particular behavior.

- Tape record your read-alouds of poems for children to hear independently.

- Make every moment a language-learning experience! Reread or recite favorite poems during regrouping times or while children are waiting for another activity.

- Focus Talk around a familiar poem anywhere, any time!

Phonics Link Activities

Children who have practice hearing and saying the individual sounds of language are well prepared to meet those sounds in print. You will want to help children learn the names of the letters before beginning phonics activities that associate familiar sounds with their corresponding letters. The use of letter cards is a good way to introduce the letter or letters that represent each sound. Blackline masters beginning on page 257 provide a template for creating letter cards for the sounds that are targeted in this book.

The following phonics activities can assist you in introducing children to the names of the letters, and in using poetry to help children associate familiar sounds of language with the letters that represent those sounds. You will want to adapt these activities for other sounds and add your own activity ideas.

Dancing Letters, Singing Sounds

Introduce or review the song "Twinkle Twinkle." Then choose a familiar language sound and introduce the letter card that represents that sound. Invite children to sing the sound of the letter(s) repeatedly to the "Twinkle Twinkle" tune as they "dance" with the letter card. For example, "lyrics" for the *wh* letter card would look like this:

wh, wh, wh, wh, wh, wh, wh

wh, wh, wh, wh, wh, wh, wh

wh, wh, wh, wh, wh, wh, wh

wh, wh, wh, wh, wh, wh, wh

wh, wh, wh, wh, wh, wh, wh

wh, wh, wh, wh, wh, wh, wh

"Dancing" might involve swinging the letter card left and right or up and down to each beat of the song. As children become more experienced, invite them to help create actual lyrics for other sounds. The prefix *dis-*, for example, might involve singing the spelling of the prefix, as well as its sound and meaning to the tune of "Twinkle Twinkle":

D-i-s says *dis, dis, dis*

Dis, dis, dis, dis, dis, dis, dis

Dis is a prefix, it means *not;*

I hear *dis* in words a lot.

In *dislike, discharge, disappear,*

When I hear *dis*, then *not* is clear.

You may want to talk about how the traditional "ABC Song" and "Twinkle Twinkle" share the same tune.

Lift It!

Provide each child with a letter card representing the sound of final blend *-ft*. Read aloud or recite "Fifty Nifty Soldiers," "A Lift," or "A Carelessly Crafted Raft." Invite children to "lift" their *-ft* letter cards each time they hear the final blend's sound in the poem. Once children are familiar with the poem's words, you might pause during the read-aloud so that children can say the sound of *-ft* as they "lift" their letter cards.

OW!

Introduce or review "Scowling Owl," "The Sound of the Wind," or "Under the Ground." During a repeated reading, ask children to say "OW!" and show their *ou/ow* letter cards every time they hear the sound of *ou/ow* as in *out/cow*. Adapt the activity so that children say "SPLENDID!" or "SPLASH!" each time they hear the *spl* sound as you read "Splish Splash Rain" or "A Splurge." Other adaptations might include the following: "WHEE!" for the *wh* sound in "Whirly Wheels" and "Whoosh!," "SH-H-H!" for the *sh* sound in "Posing," "Sheepshape," or "Ocean Magic," or "ASTOUNDING!" for the final blend *-nd* in "Yolanda the Panda" or "An Astounding Legend." Invite children to suggest exclamatory words for other sounds.

Blending to Rhyme

Once children know the sounds of consonant digraphs, invite them to put the sounds before little words, such as *in, at, eat,* and *air*, to make a rhyming-word family for each little word. For example, children might say "wheat, cheat, sheet." Children will enjoy telling you which of their new words are real words they might hear in "book talk" and "talk talk" and which, if any, words are nonsense words.

Rhyme Time

Creating lists of rhyming-word families is a fun activity that encourages children to hear and say a particular sound. Start by saying three rhyming words, such as *think, pink,* and *drink*. Have children add real and coined words to the rhyming-word family until they are out of sug-

gestions. Record the words in a list, highlight the real words, and help children use a dictionary to check any questionable words. Repeat for other rhyming-word families, such as *lamp, stamp, damp; very, Larry, hairy; sort, sport, report;* and *power, tower, hour.*

Invite children to create sentences that include four or more words from any one rhyming-word family. At another time, have children coin a creature's name that rhymes with a list of words, then illustrate the creature and add its name to the list. Finally, try adding *y* as *e* or word endings, such as *-d* or *-ed, -ing, -est,* or *-er,* to words in a rhyming-word family list. Which new words are real words?

Tongue Twisters

Introduce or review "Charlie's Chickens," "Striped Straps," "Doublethink," and "The Third Throw." Talk about the sound that's heard again and again in each poem and the tongue-twister effect. Then share tongue-twister sentences such as the following and invite children to create others:

Thelma's thankful for Theodore's thoughtful thoughts.

A wholloping whale whacked a whalloping whack!

Sing a springy song of spring.

Roy enjoys toiling with loyal royals.

Clap and Stomp

Show the *th* letter card and remind children of the letter's sound. Ask children to listen for the sound of *th* as you read "Brother" or

"TogeTHer." Then cite a word from the poem that contains the *th* sound. Help children determine whether the sound occurs at the beginning, middle, or end of the word. Encourage the use of a dictionary to check the word. Then, invite children to clap out the beats of the word and *stomp* for the syllable that contains the sound of *th*. For example, the pattern for *birthday* would be STOMP—CLAP. Repeat for other words containing the sound of *th*. Adapt the activity for other sounds.

Stretch and Shrink

Children enjoy stretching out familiar words to exaggerate each individual sound. Practice stretching some of the following little words that contain the sounds of short and long vowels: NO, YES, NOT, STOP, RED, GO, POP, DAD, MOM. Have children repeat each stretched-out word and then "shrink" the word to say it as they might hear it in "book talk" and "talk talk." Then encourage children to try longer words such as *lightning, yellow, window, address, bedtime, body, plant,* or *remind.*

Blends and Friends

Invite children to be "final blends friends," "three-letter friends," or "short vowel friends." Ask children to stand and hold their respective letter cards. Have children take turns to think of a word that includes their own letter card's sound, and then "blend" the word by joining hands with "friends" whose letter cards help to complete the word. Have "friends" drop hands, say their letter card's sound, and then join hands again, blending the sounds to say the word. Children who are not holding letter cards at the time might record the words. Challenge children to see how many words they can make. Repeat the activity to have children build words that include other sounds, such as long vowels, other vowel sounds, word endings, and consonant digraphs.

Coining Words

Ask children to listen for made-up or coined words as you read aloud "Introduction" or "Chipmunkskunkdonkmonkey." Then focus on a particular sound and invite children to coin other words by either combining words or parts of words as Richard Michelson did in "Chipmunkskunkdonkmonkey," or by adding endings or suffixes to words as William Cole did in "Introduction."

Hink-Pinks and Hinky-Pinkys

Show children how rhyming-word pairs can be linked to create humorous or unusual ideas called hink-pinks and hinky-pinkys. Hink-pinks are two one-syllable rhyming words, such as *kink link, damp champ,* and *large barge;* hinky-pinkys are two two-syllable rhyming words, such as *sneezer pleaser, fender bender,* and *stable cable.*

Consonant Digraphs

ch as in *chin*
sh as in *ship*
th as in *thank*
th as in *this*
wh as in *why*

ch

Charlie's Chickens

by
Babs Bell Hajdusiewicz

TARGETED SOUND

Consonant digraph **ch** as in **chin**:

Charlie's, chickens, Charlie, Chip, chunky, chicken, choose, champion, charmed, chant, champions, chunks, chitlins, chilled, cheddar, cheese, charming

ADDITIONAL SOUNDS

R-controlled vowel **ar** as in **park**:

Charlie's, Charlie, charmed, charming

Short vowel **i** as in **pin**:

chickens, Chip, chicken, his, with, into, chitlins, chilled

FOCUSING TALK

■ Read or recite the poem while eating soup. Talk about different kinds of soup and ingredients each might include.

■ Personalize the poem by substituting children's names and other kinds of soup and food items in the poem.

ACTIVITY: CHOOSING CHILLY CHEWIES

Invite children to use chopsticks to choose "chilly" chewy snacks, such as cheese chunks or chocolate chips, from a tray. Some children will enjoy the extra challenge of changing to their nondominant hands to try the chopsticks.

LISTEN! LISTEN! HEAR THAT SOUND?

Initial	Medial	Final
channel	itchy	hopscotch
chapter	matching	March
cheap	merchant	much
cherish	pitcher	screech
chore	purchase	search
church	stitches	stitch
	watched	

Charlie's Chickens

Charlie Chip was hungry
For some chunky chicken soup
So he went to choose a chicken
From his champion chicken coop.

But Charlie's champion chickens
Charmed poor Charlie with a chant,
"You can't make champions into chunks!
You can't!
You can't!
You can't!"

So Charlie Chip serves chitlins
With chilled chunks of cheddar cheese
While his charming champion chickens chant,
"Charlie, pass the peas!"

Babs Bell Hajdusiewicz

Consonant Digraphs:

c h

ch

The Search

by
Heather Osborne

TARGETED SOUND

Consonant digraph **ch** as in **chin:**

search, searched, checkered, chair, Cheerios®, chess, charm, chocolate, chip, chunk, cheese, chalk, chewed-up, channel, changer

ADDITIONAL SOUNDS

R-controlled vowels/vowel digraphs:

search, searched, chair, there, were, Cheerios®, charm

Short vowels:

inside, checkered, it, hidden, but, chess, man, and, that, chocolate, chip, chunk, of, chewed-up, channel

FOCUSING TALK

▪ Tell about a search you've embarked on and whether or not you found what you were seeking. As you talk about your experience, use synonyms such as *pursue, seek,* or *anticipate* for *searched,* and *discover, uncover,* or *locate* for *found.*

▪ When searching for an object, orally list the other things you're finding as you look for the wanted item. Children will eagerly help you name all the things you *aren't* seeking! In addition to adding to children's vocabulary, you'll be modeling a helpful way to avoid becoming impatient or frustrated during a search.

ACTIVITY: CHANNEL CHANGERS

Help children cut a rectangle from cardboard or polystyrene foam. Provide a channel changer for children to consult as they use markers to write numbers and other symbols on the foam or on paper squares.

LISTEN! LISTEN! HEAR THAT SOUND?

Initial	Medial	Final
chain	exchange	attach
chalk	matches	catch
challenge	nacho	inch
champion	searching	reach
chance	stitches	stretch
charge	teacher	such
		touch

The Search

I searched inside our checkered chair.
I thought I'd find it hidden there.

But all I found were
Cheerios®
a chess man
and a charm that glows
a chocolate chip
a chunk of cheese
a piece of chalk
two chewed-up peas.

I searched inside the checkered chair
but found *no* channel changer there.

Heather Osborne

Consonant Digraphs:

ch

sh

sh
Posing

by
Adelaide B. Shaw

sh

sh

sh

sh

sh

TARGETED SOUND

Consonant digraph **sh** as in **ship:**

washed, brushed, shined, shoes, short, flashbulbs, flashed, shutters, shooting's, finished, slush

ADDITIONAL SOUND

Ending **-d/-ed** as in **hoped/waited:**

washed, brushed, shined, slicked, posed, flashed, clicked, relaxed, finished

FOCUSING TALK

▪ You'll want to quote lines from this poem when school photographs are being taken. Children will also enjoy hearing stories about times when you've had to pose for photographs.

▪ Share old photos or use books or magazines that contain old photos. Talk about how the subjects of the photos may have felt as they prepared for the "shoot" or while actually posing. This is a good time to help children recognize that although most of us don't enjoy the preparation in having our photos taken, the memories are valuable to us later.

ACTIVITY: SHADOW POSES

Have children work in pairs to create each other's silhouettes. Attach paper to a wall and have one child pose sideways between the paper and a strong light source. The partner can draw around the child's shadow. Later, help children trace around their images on black paper, cut out the silhouettes, and glue onto white paper.

LISTEN! LISTEN! HEAR THAT SOUND?

Initial	Medial	Final
shop	motion	rosebush
short	slushy	rush
show	sushi	splash
shut	tissue	toothbrush
shy	Tricia	
surely	wished	

Posing

I washed and brushed and shined my shoes.
My hair was short and slicked.
I stood and posed while flashbulbs flashed
And shutters clicked and clicked.

Now I'm relaxed.
The shooting's done.
I'm finished for today.
It's back to dirt and mud and slush.
I like myself that way.

Adelaide B. Shaw

Consonant Digraphs:

sh

sh

sh

Sheepshape

by
X. J. Kennedy

sh

sh

sh

sh

sh

TARGETED SOUND

Consonant digraph **sh** as in **ship:**

> sheepshape, shear, sheep, shapes, shooting, short, shears, shilly-shally, sheer, shaggy, shave

ADDITIONAL SOUNDS

Long vowels:

> sheepshape, I, sheep, shapes, like, shooting, apes, my, ewe, right, two, valley, make, me, don't, shilly-shally, wiry, worthwhile, to, save, oh, shave

Other consonant digraphs:

> them, the, with, their, worthwhile, what

FOCUSING TALK

▪ After enjoying this poem, you'll want to refer to scissors as "shears" and a child's new haircut as "shorn locks." Ask children which "shearing shops" they visit when they need haircuts.

▪ Children will enjoy hearing you use the poem's expression "shilly-shally" to mean "mess around" or "waste time."

ACTIVITY: SHEARED SHAPES

Have children cut out cardboard circles, squares, or other shapes. Provide cotton balls or fiberfill that children can glue onto their shapes. Help children use scissors to shear designs into their shapes.

LISTEN! LISTEN! HEAR THAT SOUND?

Initial	Medial	Final
shake	admission	crash
shape	delicious	dish
sheet	discussion	establish
shell	pollution	flash
shirt		
shoe		

Sheepshape

I shear sheep in all sorts of shapes
Like shooting stars and spangles.
I shear them in the shapes of apes.
My ewe has four right angles.

I give some sheep a camel's back,
Two mountains and a valley.
I make short shrift of them with shears.
Me, I don't shilly-shally.

I shear sheep short. Their wiry wool
Is well worthwhile to save.
Oh, what sheer joy it is to give
A shaggy sheep a shave!

X. J. Kennedy

Consonant Digraphs:

sh

sh

Ocean Magic

by
Bonnie Kerr Morris

TARGETED SOUND

Consonant digraph **sh** as in **ship:**

> ocean, seashell, shiny, shore-shaped, wave-crashed, wash, polish, show, wish, sun-splashed, share

ADDITIONAL SOUNDS

Long vowels:

> ocean, I, seashell, shiny, shore-shaped, sides, I'd, wave-crashed, tides, to, show, each, rainbow, hue, make, days, you

Short vowels:

> magic, if, seashell, with, listen, as, it, whispered, of, wave-crashed, summer, and, polish, then, wish, sun-splashed, them

FOCUSING TALK

- Use the different meanings of *shell* in conversation: an outer covering, a home for a plant or an animal, the act of removing an outer covering, a sleeveless blouse without a collar, a shape of pasta, or a thin layer of pastry as in a pie shell.

- Share the tongue-twister rhyme that begins "She sells seashells by the seashore. . . ." Then substitute names beginning with *sh,* such as Shawanda, Sharon, Shelly, or Shawn, in the rhyme.

ACTIVITY: A SHELL FOR TREASURES

Provide small boxes with lids, such as jewelry or gift boxes and oatmeal boxes, along with peanuts or walnuts. Allow children to help shell the nuts and then glue the shells onto the outside of a box and lid to make a special "home" for keepsakes. Add paint or glitter as desired. At another time, repeat the activity using eggshells.

LISTEN! LISTEN! HEAR THAT SOUND?

Initial	Medial	Final
shall	ashes	fresh
Sharon	bushes	goldfish
she	cautious	mash
ship	education	push
	friendship	

Ocean Magic

If I found a seashell,
    with shiny shore-shaped sides,
I'd listen as it whispered sounds
    of wave-crashed summer tides.

I'd wash it off and polish it,
    to show each rainbow hue,
Then make a wish for sun-splashed days
    and share them all with you.

Bonnie Kerr Morris

Consonant Digraphs:

sh

th

th

Toothpaste

by
Stan Lee Werlin

TARGETED SOUND

Consonant digraph unvoiced **th** as in **thank:**

toothpaste, bathtub, north, south, mouth

ADDITIONAL SOUNDS

Consonant digraph voiced **th** as in **this:**

there, the

Consonant **t** as in **top:**

toothpaste, it, got, toilet, what, bathtub, it's, time, except

Long vowels:

toothpaste, my, nose, rows, pj's, you, gooey, overflowing, congealing, ceiling, time, I, squeeze, sprays, almost, inside

FOCUSING TALK

■ Substitute *mouthwash* for *toothpaste*. Another time, innovate on the poem's text to describe a baby's messy eating habits: "There is *pudding* on *his* fingers. . . ."

■ Children will enjoy hearing you tell the poem's story as if it were a story rather than a poem.

ACTIVITY: THIRTY-TWO TRUTHS ABOUT TEETH

Provide thirty-two toothbrushes, one for each tooth children will have when they are grown. Display the toothbrushes on a bulletin board or stand them on a polystyrene foam base. Help children make a list of facts about teeth, such as teeth are white, baby teeth fall out, teeth are covered with enamel, teeth need to be brushed, teeth have roots, etc. Then help children write each fact as if a toothbrush were telling the fact. For example, a toothbrush might say, "I keep teeth clean." Attach a caption to each toothbrush.

LISTEN! LISTEN! HEAR THAT SOUND?

Initial	Medial	Final
thank	anything	both
thankful	athlete	cloth
thatch	author	ninth
theater		
theft		

Toothpaste

There is toothpaste on my fingers.
There is toothpaste in my nose.
There is toothpaste on my mirror
in a hundred squiggly rows.

There is toothpaste on my pj's,
how it got there you can guess.
There are gobs of gooey toothpaste
in the toilet, what a mess.

There is toothpaste in the bathtub,
overflowing on the floor.
It's congealing on the ceiling
and it's dripping down the door.

Every time I squeeze the toothpaste,
it sprays north and west and south.
There is toothpaste almost everywhere,
except inside my mouth!

Stan Lee Werlin

Consonant Digraphs:

th

th

Doublethink

by
Jeff Moss

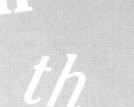

TARGETED SOUND

Consonant digraph unvoiced **th** as in **thank:**

doublethink, think, thought, thoughtful, thoughts

ADDITIONAL SOUNDS

Final blend **-nk** as in **pink:**

doublethink, think

Vowel **a** as in **ball/ought/claw:**

thought, thoughtful, thoughts

 FOCUSING TALK

▪ Children will enjoy hearing you quote the poem when you or a child is deep in thought. When someone seems to need some quiet time, mention that some "think time" or "doublethink time" is in order.

▪ Introduce the idea of "triplethink" or "quadruplethink." In the latter case, change the word *three* to *four* and complete the rhyme with a line such as: "Do those thoughts think up more?"

 ACTIVITY: I'LL THINK A THOUGHT

Talk about how helpful a positive thought can be. Then help children illustrate or write a positive thought on a paper thought-bubble. Children can post their "thoughts" in special places.

 LISTEN! LISTEN! HEAR THAT SOUND?

Initial	Medial	Final
therapy	athletic	bath
thermometer	bathtub	death
thick	faithful	north
thing	truthful	sixth
think		south

Doublethink

I think I thought some thoughtful thoughts.
I think I thought up three.
But now I think about those thoughts:
Do those thoughts think of me?

Jeff Moss

The Thinker

by
Babs Bell Hajdusiewicz

TARGETED SOUND

Consonant digraph unvoiced **th** as in **thank:**

thinker, thinking, thought, think

ADDITIONAL SOUNDS

R-controlled vowels/vowel digraphs:

surely, for, more, four-hundred, years, figured

Short vowel **i** as in **pin:**

thinker, his, is, difficult, thinking, if, think, figured, it

FOCUSING TALK

▪ To innovate on the poem's text, you might strike a thoughtful pose and say, "My problem is truly a difficult one. Here's what I am thinking about. . . ." You need not follow the poem's rhythm as you go on to tell children about your thought.

▪ Quote the poem's first two lines whenever you observe a child who's deep in thought. Share Auguste Rodin's sculpture titled *The Thinker.*

ACTIVITY: OUR THOUGHTS

Invite children to bring in photographs of themselves and their pets for a "thoughtful" display. Provide white paper cut in the shape of thought-bubbles and help children write or illustrate a thought that might accompany each photo.

LISTEN! LISTEN! HEAR THAT SOUND?

Initial	Medial	Final
theme	nothing	teeth
thigh	python	truth
thirsty	something	with
thirty	toothbrush	worth
thought		wrath

The Thinker

His problem is surely a difficult one.
What *can* he be thinking about?
If *I* thought for more than four-hundred years,
I think *I'd* have figured it out.

Babs Bell Hajdusiewicz

Consonant Digraphs:

th

Brother

by

Mary Ann Hoberman

TARGETED SOUND

Consonant digraph voiced **th** as in **this:**

brother, mother, another, bother, father, brother's

ADDITIONAL SOUNDS

R-controlled vowel **ur** as in **hurt:**

brother, mother, another, bother, father, brother's

Schwa **o** as in **lemon:**

brother, mother, another, brother's

FOCUSING TALK

▪ Children who have sisters will enjoy hearing *sister* substituted in the poem. For children who have older siblings, substitute *bigger* for *little* throughout the poem. Children will be eager to join in on the tongue-twister effect when this poem is read rapidly. At other times, try reading the poem so as to emphasize the *th* or *-er* sound.

▪ Use the words *bother, bothering, bothered,* and *bothersome* as you talk about things that bother you and ways you've found to deal with bothersome situations. You may also want to use the familiar exclamation, "Oh, brother!" as you talk about bothersome things.

ACTIVITY: OH, BROTHER, WHAT A BOTHER!

Invite children to draw or cut out pictures to illustrate situations that bother them. Have children work with partners to share and talk about their pictures, an experience that can help them recognize that someone else may feel the same way they do, and that frustration can often be alleviated simply by talking about it with someone. You may want to have children compile their pictures to make a book.

LISTEN! LISTEN! HEAR THAT SOUND?

Initial		Medial	Final
than	then	breathing	smooth
that	therefore	farther	
their	they	gather	
them		leather	
		northern	
		together	

Brother

I had a little brother
And I brought him to my mother
And I said I want another
Little brother for a change.
But she said don't be a bother
So I took him to my father
And I said this little bother
Of a brother's very strange.
But he said one little brother
Is exactly like another
And every little brother
Misbehaves a bit he said.
So I took the little bother
From my mother and my father
And I put the little bother
Of a brother back to bed.

Mary Ann Hoberman

th

th

TogeTHer

by

Babs Bell Hajdusiewicz

th

th

th

th

TARGETED SOUND

Consonant digraph voiced **th** as in **this:**

> together, they, there, this, that, these, those, then, them, they're, than, the, their, theirs, therefore, thus, though, other

ADDITIONAL SOUNDS

Consonant digraph unvoiced **th** as in **thank:**

> thing, think

Short vowels:

> together, and, in, this, that, then, them, than, thus, but, thing, think

FOCUSING TALK

■ As you and children work together, innovate on the poem's text to say, "We work together, you and I, to. . . ." or "You work together, (children's names), to. . . ."

■ Recite the poem, substituting words from the lists below.

ACTIVITY: THEY GO TOGETHER

Have children draw or cut out pictures of objects or ideas that typically go together. Examples may include a comb and brush, kisses and hugs, a ball and glove, left and right, thunder and lightning, king and queen, boys and girls, and stop and go.

LISTEN! LISTEN! HEAR THAT SOUND?

Initial	Medial	Final
that's	although	lathe
the	bother	smooth
themselves	clothing	soothe
there	either	
there'll	father	
	mother	
	weather	

T o g e T H e r

They work together
T and *H*
to make one sound in *there,*
and *this*
and *that*
and *these*
and *those*
and *then*
and *them*
and *they're*.

And *than*
and *the*
and *their*
and *theirs*
and *therefore,*
thus and *though*.
But *T* and *H* work other ways
in *thing*, and *think*, and *throw!*

Babs Bell Hajdusiewicz

Consonant Digraphs:

th

wh
Whirly Wheels

by
Katherine Burton

TARGETED SOUND

Consonant digraph **wh** as in **why:**

> whirly, wheels, what, whizzy, whirring, whistling, wheeling, while, whisper, whip, whoop, whup

ADDITIONAL SOUNDS

Consonant **l** as in **long:**

> whirly, wheels, feeling, whistling, wheeling, while

Ending **-ing** as in **going:**

> feeling, whirring, whistling, wheeling

Long vowel **e** as in **me:**

> wheels, feeling, wheeling

FOCUSING TALK

▪ The poem's second stanza might be quoted when watching any wheels in motion. Similarly, the words *Whip, Whoop? Whup!* can well describe someone's surprise during or after a spill.

▪ Quote the poem's first stanza when children talk about feeling dizzy from spinning around. Then innovate on the text to say, "What a whizzy, dizzy feeling!" or "What a mixed-up, funny feeling!"

ACTIVITY: SNACKS ON WHEELS

Provide candy lifesavers and carrot, celery, or pretzel sticks for children to use as wheels and axles. Cheese bits or miniature marshmallows might double as "fill" in the holes. Provide lettuce or cabbage leaves that children can lay over four wheels as a wagon bed. Children might fill their "wagons" with cereal or another snack food.

LISTEN! LISTEN! HEAR THAT SOUND?

Initial	Medial
whale	anywhere
when	cartwheel
where	overwhelm
which	two-wheeler
whistle	

Whirly Wheels

What a
whizzy,
whirly feeling!

Wheels are
whirring
whistling
wheeling
while they whisper,

    Whip!
Whoop?
    Whup!

Wheeling down . . .
not wheeling up.

Katherine Burton

wh

WHOOSH!

by
Babs Bell Hajdusiewicz

TARGETED SOUND

Consonant digraph **wh** as in **why:**

> whoosh, whenever, when, which, what, why, where, whistle, wheel, while, whale, white, wheat, whew

ADDITIONAL SOUNDS

Long vowels:

> whoosh, I, say, why, I'm, wheel, while, whale, white, wheat, okay, who

Short vowels:

> whenever, when, which, as, if, whistle, of, in, and, but, that's, huff

FOCUSING TALK

- Once children are familiar with the poem, read it rapidly, encouraging children to chime in on "Whew!" Model substituting other *wh* words, such as *whop, whee, whir, whisk,* or *whiz.*

- Create a parody that gives listeners a surprise ending with an innovation such as "I'll HUFF when I say, 'I'll blow your house down!'"

ACTIVITY: WHOOSH AND HUFF

Help children write each of the poem's *wh* words on a small square of lightweight paper. Slightly fold the papers and then stand them on a tabletop. When children place their mouths very close to a "whoosh" word and say the word, the whoosh of air should blow the word down, while "huff" words, such as *who, whole, whoever,* or *whom,* should remain standing.

LISTEN! LISTEN! HEAR THAT SOUND?

Initial	Medial
wheeze	awhile
whether	meanwhile
whimper	nowhere
whirly	somewhat
whistling	

WHOOSH!

Whenever I say
when or *which*
or *what* or *why*
or *where*
I WHOOSH as if I'm gonna whistle
 WHOOSH
a WHOOSH of air!

More WHOOSH
in *wheel* and *while*
and *whale* and *white*
and *wheat* and . . .

W
    H
       E
          W!

I'm out of WHOOSH!
But that's okay—
I'll HUFF when I say *who*.

Babs Bell Hajdusiewicz

Consonant Digraphs:

w h

Final Blends

-ft as in *left*

-mp as in *lamp*

-nd as in *and*

-ng as in *sing*

-nk as in *pink*

-nt as in *ant*

ft

A Lift

by
Dee Lillegard

TARGETED SOUND

Final blend **-ft** as in **left:**

> lift, raft, nifty, drifty, craft, swift, drift

ADDITIONAL SOUNDS

Consonant **l** as in **long:**

> lift, lying

Short vowel **i** as in **pin:**

> lift, river, nifty, drifty, isn't swift, drift

FOCUSING TALK

- You'll find many opportunities to use the poem's -*ft* words as you converse with children. Use *nifty* to describe children's creations, *drift* in place of *come* or *go*, the noun or verb forms of *craft* for *make* or *artwork*, and *swift* or *swiftly* to describe children's quickness.

- This poem lends itself to setting the mood for a quiet time. Have children close their eyes and imagine lying on a raft as they pretend to softly drift up and down. At another time, suggest a tempo change as you innovate on the second stanza to say, "The river's kinda swift!"

ACTIVITY: NIFTY LIFTING

Help children discover ways to move a scrap of paper from one spot to another without touching it with their hand. Children might blow on the paper, fan the paper, use a suction cup, glue, or tape, or flip the paper upward with a stick.

LISTEN! LISTEN! HEAR THAT SOUND?

Medial	Final
after	draft
afternoon	fluffed
softest	left
	thrift

A Lift

Lift me.
Lift me.
Put me on a raft.
Send me down the river
    on a nifty drifty craft.

Lift me.
Lift me.
The river isn't swift.
Lying on a river raft,
    I drift . . .
        drift . . .
        drift.

Dee Lillegard

Final Blends:

ft

ft

Fifty Nifty Soldiers

by
Heidi Roemer

TARGETED SOUND

Final blend **-ft** as in **left:**

> fifty, nifty, buffed, puffed, scoffed, coughed, swiftly, shifted, drifted, sifted, lifted

ADDITIONAL SOUNDS

Ending **-d/ed** as in **hoped/waited:**

> waited, heeded, shifted, drifted, sifted, lifted

Plural **-s/-es/-ies** as in **dogs/boxes/babies:**

> soldiers, boots, chests, push-ups, bodies, sands, faces, hands, arms, G. I. Joes, rows

Short vowel **i** as in **pin:**

> fifty, nifty, stiffly, hill, drill, swiftly, shifted, drifted, in, sifted, lifted, cliff

Suffix **-ly** as in **lonely:**

> stiffly, patiently, swiftly

FOCUSING TALK

▪ Use the poem's words "None scoffed. None coughed" to describe children waiting in a line. Similarly, when picking up your children from another activity, comment that you've "plucked your twenty nifty kids."

▪ Children will enjoy hearing some of the poem's words, such as *buffed, puffed, scoffed, drifted, heeded,* and *plucked,* used in other contexts.

ACTIVITY: NIFTY SIFTING

Provide a flour sifter, flour, and measuring spoons and cup. Invite children to compare an amount of flour, before and after sifting. Encourage children to compare the flour's texture before and after sifting, as well.

LISTEN! LISTEN! HEAR THAT SOUND?

Medial	Final
crafty	craft
drifting	drift
sifter	gift
thrifty	soft

Fifty Nifty Soldiers

Fifty nifty soldiers stood there stiffly on the hill.

> Boots buffed.
> Chests puffed.

Fifty nifty soldiers waited patiently to drill.

> None scoffed.
> None coughed.

"Fifty push-ups!" Swiftly, soldiers heeded the command.

> Bodies shifted.
> Sands drifted.

Fifty nifty soldiers lay with faces in the sand.

> Hands sifted.
> Arms lifted.

From the sandy cliff, I plucked my fifty G.I. Joes
And lined my fifty soldiers
once again,
in nifty rows.

Heidi Roemer

Final Blends:

ft

ft

A Carelessly Crafted Raft

by
Lucinda Cave

TARGETED SOUND

Final blend **-ft** as in **left:**

crafted, raft, hefty, draft, swiftly, shifted, raft, luffed, drifted, afterwards, aft

ADDITIONAL SOUNDS

Ending **-d/-ed** as in **hoped/waited:** crafted, shifted, luffed, drifted, crashed

Other blends: crafted, draft, wind, swiftly, drifted, crashed

Short vowel **a** as in **cat:** crafted, raft, draft, and, afterwards, crashed, aft

Short vowel **i** as in **pin:** in, wind, swiftly, shifted, drifted, its

Suffix **-ly** as in **lonely:** carelessly, swiftly

FOCUSING TALK

▪ Use the poem's phrase *carelessly crafted* to talk about a garment or other item that's falling apart. Similarly, refer to a well-made item or a child's project as having been "carefully crafted."

▪ Refer to lunch as a "hefty" meal, a rush of cold air as a "draft," or say "swiftly shifted" to talk about any quick change. Talk about the "aft," or rear end of a ship or an airplane. Tell children that when a raft "luffs," it moves into the wind.

ACTIVITY: WELL-CRAFTED RAFTS?

Provide glue and craft sticks, straws, balsam scraps, plastic lids, and cardboard for children to use in constructing rafts. Encourage children to launch their rafts in a sink or tub of water to discover which materials and construction methods produce a "carefully crafted raft" or a "carelessly crafted raft."

LISTEN! LISTEN! HEAR THAT SOUND?

Medial	Final
nifty	loft
shifting	sift
	soft
	stuffed
	tuft

A Carelessly Crafted Raft

A carelessly crafted raft
was caught in a hefty draft.
    The wind swiftly shifted.
    The raft luffed and drifted.
And afterwards crashed on its aft.

Lucinda Cave

mp
The Champ

by
Heidi Roemer

TARGETED SOUND

Final blend **-mp** as in **lamp:** champ, Scamp, champion, camper, Kemper's, camp, simply, scampered, limped, stomped, swamps, damp, trampled, lump, tempted, complain, sympathy, slumped

ADDITIONAL SOUNDS

Ending **-d/-ed** as in **hoped/waited:** bragged, trekked, scampered, limped, stomped, trampled, stumbled, tempted, slumped, sighed

Blends: Scamp, spent, bragged, prize, trekked, swarm, scampered, trees, stomped, through, swamps, grew, trampled, stumbled, skunk, slumped, stinky

Short vowel **a** as in **cat:** champ, Scamp, champion, camper, at, camp, bragged, as, began, scampered, past, damp, trampled, ask

FOCUSING TALK

▪ Refer to the poem by calling individuals "The Champ." Innovate on the poem's first lines by inserting a child's name and an activity other than camping. For example, "(Child's name), a champion reader, read a book at lunch today" or "(Child's name), a champion runner, ran a lap around the field."

▪ Quote the poem's lines, "Though tempted to complain, he didn't ask for sympathy," when a child handles a situation well. Similarly, you might say the lines when they apply to a situation of your own!

ACTIVITY: I'M A CHAMP!

Provide red ribbon, paper scraps, safety pins, and glue for each child to use in making an award badge. Encourage children to think about their strengths, large or small, and wear their badges to commend themselves for any and all "champion" accomplishments.

LISTEN! LISTEN! HEAR THAT SOUND?

Medial	Final
compass	chimp
example	clamp
hamper	dump
pamper	hemp
sample	limp
scampi	lump
simple	shrimp

The Champ

Scamp, a champion camper,
   spent a week at Kemper's camp.
He bragged, "I'm simply sure to win
   the prize as Hiking Champ!"

The hike began; Scamp trekked along—
   into a swarm of bees!
He fell, but scampered up again
   and limped past fallen trees.

He stomped through swamps.
   His socks grew damp.
He trampled on in rain.
   He stumbled on a lump—a skunk!
Though tempted to complain—

He didn't ask for sympathy
   when he slumped into camp.
He simply held his nose and sighed,
   "I win . . . as *Stinky* Champ!"

Heidi Roemer

Final Blends:

mp

mp
Lumps

by
Judith Thurman

mp
mp
mp
mp
mp

TARGETED SOUND

Final blend **-mp** as in **lamp:**

lumps, humps, mumps, bumps, clumps, stumps, dumps

ADDITIONAL SOUNDS

Plural **-s/-es/-ies** as in **dogs/boxes/babies:**

lumps, humps, mumps, bumps, heads, mushrooms, clumps, stumps, woods, dumps, springs, beds, bites, frogs, logs

Short vowel **u** as in **rug:**

lumps, humps, mumps, bumps, mushrooms, clumps, stumps, dumps

 ### FOCUSING TALK

▪ Talk about mumps and how immunizations prevent the disease today. You may want to refer to the tale "The Princess and the Pea" as you talk about a lumpy bed or cushion. When appropriate, talk about lumps in foods, such as tapioca, gravy, or half-mashed potatoes.

▪ Model the figurative use of *lumps* and *dumps* in sayings, such as "I'll take my lumps" or "I'm down in the dumps." Talk about how dumping trash has led to the use of the words *dump* and *dumpster* for a trash pile or trash container.

 ### ACTIVITY: LUMPS NO MORE

Provide a strainer, window screen wire, or cheesecloth for children's use in transforming a lumpy mixture of mud, or flour and water, into a smooth substance. Children can simply squeeze the cheesecloth, or use an orange or a ball to press the lumpy mixture through the strainer or screen wire.

 ### LISTEN! LISTEN! HEAR THAT SOUND?

Medial	Final
attempt	champ
camping	cramp
dampen	grump
empty	jump
temperature	lamp
umpire	plump
	pump
	stomp
	thump

Lumps

Humps are lumps
and so are mumps.

Bumps make lumps
on heads.

Mushrooms grow
in clumps of lumps—
on clumps of stumps,
in woods and dumps.

Springs spring lumps
in beds.

Mosquito bites
make itchy lumps.

Frogs on logs
make twitchy lumps.

Judith Thurman

Final Blends:

m p

nd

nd

Yolanda the Panda

by
Carol Murray

TARGETED SOUND

Final blend **-nd** as in **and:**

Yolanda, panda, candy, hand, and, handy, expand

ADDITIONAL SOUNDS

Consonant **h** as in **he:**

hand, hunch, having, handy

Short vowel **a** as in **cat:**

Yolanda, panda, candy, hand, and, have, having, handy, expand

 ### FOCUSING TALK

▪ When appropriate, personalize the poem's text to comment on a food's messiness or its "tummy-expanding" abilities. For example, you might say, "It dribbles all over *my* hand," or "Having candy so handy is making *my* tummy expand."

▪ Children will enjoy your reference to the poem when you substitute its words, "I have a hunch . . . ," for "I think" or "I believe."

 ### ACTIVITY: AN EXPANDED PANDA

Provide a copy of a picture of a panda from a book or magazine. Lay the picture over a sheet of blank paper and help children cut around the panda to have two panda shapes. Children can staple around the edges to attach the shapes, leaving a small opening. Have children "expand" the panda's tummy by stuffing it with tissue paper or cotton batting. Staple the opening shut.

 ### LISTEN! LISTEN! HEAR THAT SOUND?

Medial	Final
dandy	land
trendy	mind
wander	planned
window	pond
wonder	pound
	sand

Yolanda the Panda

Yolanda, the Panda,
slurps candy for lunch.
It dribbles all over her hand.
And I have a hunch
having candy so handy
is making her tummy expand.

Carol Murray

nd

nd

An Astounding Legend

by
Lucinda Cave

nd

nd

nd

nd

nd

TARGETED SOUND

Final blend **-nd** as in **and:**

> astounding, legend, around, bend, and, beyond, found, island, pond, sand, ground, yonder, end, mound, blend, wonder, grand, grandest, diamond, land

ADDITIONAL SOUND

Diphthong **ou/ow** as in **out/cow:**

> astounding, around, found, ground, mound

FOCUSING TALK

▪ Talk about legends, such as the "Legend of Sleeping Hollow" or the legend of the Loch Ness Monster. Create a new "legend," encouraging children to join in to help create the tale. You might begin this way: "In a land, there was an island. And on that island lived a. . . ."

▪ Once children are familiar with the word *astounding,* check their listening and critical-thinking skills by using the word appropriately and, occasionally, inappropriately. For example, you might use the word to comment on an especially good sandwich and then use it to describe a perfectly normal and not-at-all-unusual light or door or other object.

ACTIVITY: ASTOUNDING KINDNESSES

Help children cut paper into diamond shapes and write or illustrate on the diamonds a kind thought or an act they've done or plan to do. Provide glue and glitter for children to use in illustrating their "diamonds." Display the "Astounding Kindnesses" or provide safety pins so that children can wear their "diamonds."

LISTEN! LISTEN! HEAR THAT SOUND?

Medial	Final
Andrew	and
blunder	banned
handy	blind
thunder	brand
under	kind
	round

An Astounding Legend

Around the bend
And just beyond,
I found an island in a pond.

And on the island,
All around,
I found some sand upon the ground.

And on the sand
At yonder end,
I found a mound of golden blend.

And on the mound,
A wonder grand—
The grandest diamond in the land.

Lucinda Cave

Final Blends:

n d

ng

ng

Ode to Spring

by
Walter R. Brooks

ng

ng

ng

ng

ng

TARGETED SOUND

Final blend **-ng** as in **sing:**

> spring, thing, sing, king

ADDITIONAL SOUND

Short vowel **i** as in **pin:**

> spring, thing, sing, king

FOCUSING TALK

▪ Innovate on the poem's text to exclaim about other seasons. Children will especially enjoy your innovating on the text to express appreciation for them: "O (child's name), O (child's name), You wonderful thing!"

▪ To model the multiple meanings of *spring*, you might ask a child to "spring up," comment on a bud that is ready to "spring forth," or note that a hinge might "spring" if children hang on a cabinet or an entry door.

ACTIVITY: SPRINGY SPRING

Invite children to illustrate or cut out pictures that depict the marvels of springtime. Provide 1-inch by 11-inch strips of paper and show children how to fold them accordion-style to form paper "springs." Children can attach "springs" to the back of each picture and display them on a table or bulletin board.

LISTEN! LISTEN! HEAR THAT SOUND?

Medial	Final
anger	along
angle	king
bangle	lung
finger	ring
jingle	sting
single	strong
triangle	thing
	wrong

Ode to Spring

O spring, O spring,
You wonderful thing!
O spring, O spring, O spring!
O spring, O spring,
When the birdies sing
I feel like a king,
    O spring!

Walter R. Brooks

Final Blends:

n g

ng

ng
Ping-Pong Song

by
Babs Bell Hajdusiewicz

TARGETED SOUND
Final blend **-ng** as in **sing:**
> Ping-Pong, sings, song, ping, pong, long

ADDITIONAL SOUNDS
Consonant **p** as in **pet:**
> Ping-Pong, ping, pong

Short vowel **i** as in **pin:**
> ping, it, sings, ping

 ### FOCUSING TALK
- Children enjoy any and all experiences with onomatopoeia, or words that imitate a sound, such as *woof, oomphf, rrr-ip,* etc. To focus on words with the *-ng* sound, you might say, "Bing bang" when a door shuts noisily, "clingety clang" when a bell sounds, or "rrrr-ing" when a phone rings.

- Innovate on the poem's text to say, "The telephone, it sings a song as it goes RING! RING! all day long," or "The basketball, it sings a song as it goes bounce, bounce all game long."

 ### ACTIVITY: HANGING CHIMES
Help children use string and tape and a clothes hanger to make a hanging chime. Use Ping Pong balls for a chime that goes "ping-pong," nuts and bolts for a "bing-bang" chime, or old knives, forks, or spoons for a "cling-clang" chime.

 ### LISTEN! LISTEN! HEAR THAT SOUND?

Medial	Final
bingo	bang
Congo	clang
flamingo	hang
length	hung
longer	sang
tingle	song
	string
	wing

Ping-Pong Song

The Ping-Pong ball
it sings a song
as it goes
PING!
PONG!
all game long.

Babs Bell Hajdusiewicz

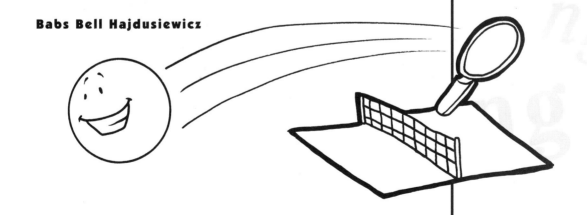

Final Blends:

n g

nk
Skink and Skunk

by Lucinda Cave

TARGETED SOUND

Final blend -**nk** as in **pink:**

> skink, skunk, bank, drinking, drink, think, drank, stink, rank, wink, stinks, kerplunk

ADDITIONAL SOUNDS

Blend **sc/sk** as in **scare/sky:**

> skink, skunk

Short vowel **i** as in **pin:**

> skink, river, drinking, drink, think, stink, quizzed, with, wink, flipped, emitted, stinks, in

FOCUSING TALK

▪ Children will enjoy your innovating on the text as you meet them "in the hall at the fountain while drinking a drink."

▪ The word *emitted* will be interesting to children as you talk about someone who has emitted a howl, or a volcano that emitted lava. Obviously, children will be eager to join you in saying, "I'm outta here!" at the end of a school day.

ACTIVITY: STINKY BOOK

Talk about how some smells, such as perfumes or food smells, may be thought of as fragrances *or* stinky smells, depending on the "smeller's" preference or sensitivity. Have children draw or cut out pictures of stinky things, such as a skunk, broccoli or cabbage cooking, a soiled diaper, an unclean bathroom, smoke, or a garbage can. Staple sheets of paper together so as to make a book and have children arrange their pictures on the left-hand pages. Help children write a phrase such as "I smell something stinky in the (location). I smell . . ." on the right-hand pages. Children will enjoy predicting the picture they'll see when they turn each page.

LISTEN! LISTEN! HEAR THAT SOUND?

Medial	Final
crinkle	bank
sphinx	link
sprinkler	pink
twinkle	spank
winked	tank

Skink and Skunk

A skink met a skunk
and a skunk met a skink
on the bank of a river
while drinking a drink.

"I think," said the skink,
to the skunk, as they drank,

"You might make a stink
and a stink would smell rank."

"Who? Me?" quizzed the skunk,
to the skink with a wink.
Then Skunk flipped her tail
and emitted a stink.

"That stinks!" shrieked the skink.
"I am outta here, Skunk!"
Skink leaped in the river—
Kersplash!
And kerplunk!

Lucinda Cave

Final Blends:

n k

nk

nk

Chipmunk- skunkdonk- monkey

by
Richard Michelson

TARGETED SOUND

Final blend **-nk** as in **pink:**

Chipmunkskunkdonkmonkey, chipmunk, skunk, thinks, stunk, donkey, monkey, spunky

ADDITIONAL SOUNDS

S-blends: Chipmunkskunkdonkmonkey, skunk, stunk, stubborn, spunky

Short vowel **u** as in **rug:** Chipmunkskunkdonkmonkey, chipmunk, skunk, nutty, stunk, mother, monkey, stubborn, spunky, nutty

FOCUSING TALK

▪ Children will enjoy hearing you quote the poem's last stanza, especially when you've made a mistake or when you're not feeling quite like yourself.

▪ Mix up the poem's title in other ways, such as "Monkskunkdonkey" or "Chipdonkskunkdonkmonkey." Children will perk up when you create humorous images by combining other words or parts of words. Examples might include a human-looking animal as in *animan,* a combination of *write* and *print* as in *wrint,* or a puzzling math problem as in *arithmetricker.*

ACTIVITY: FUNKY CHARACTERS

Provide old science and nature magazines for children's use in cutting out animal feet, heads, tails, trunks, etc. Have children glue parts of several animals onto construction paper to create, then name, their own unique "funky" animals. For example, an elephant's trunk, a giraffe's neck, duck feet, and a skunk's body might be combined to create a "Girunk" or a "Phirant." Children may want to add human touches, such as shoes or hats, to their animals.

LISTEN! LISTEN! HEAR THAT SOUND?

Medial	Final
donkey	blank
Duncan	chipmunk
uncle	drink
Yonkers	ink
	prank
	yank

Chipmunkskunk-
donkmonkey

My grandma is a chipmunk.
My grandpa is a skunk.
He thinks that she's half nutty.
She says he's always stunk.

My dear ol' dad's a donkey.
My mother is a monkey.
She thinks my dad is stubborn.
He thinks my mom is spunky.

Some days I'm sorta nutty
and some days I act spunky.
But I like me the way I am—
a chipmunkskunkdonkmonkey.

Richard Michelson

Final Blends:

n k

nk

Hummingbird

by
Evelyn Amuedo Wade

nk
nk
nk
nk
nk

TARGETED SOUND

Final blend **-nk** as in **pink:**

> tiddlywink, drink, pinker, pink, think, blink

ADDITIONAL SOUNDS

Consonant **p** as in **pet:**

> whips, sip, pinker, pink, zip, flip

Short vowel **i** as in **pin:**

> quick, flick, tiddlywink, whips, in, sip, drink, pinker, pink, zip, with, flip, think, blink

FOCUSING TALK

■ To comment on a child's quickness in getting a drink, say, "Quick as a flick of a tiddlywink, she whips to the hall for a sip of a drink." When you or a child eats a favorite food, say, "Before I can think, it's gone in a blink."

■ Talk about a hummingbird's attraction to red and pink. When a child wears red or pink, you might pretend the child is a hummingbird and say, "That's pinker than pink! You'll be whipping along for a sip of a drink!"

ACTIVITY: TIDDLYWINKS

Paint four flat buttons the same color for each player. Use a larger flat button as a flipper and a shallow flat metal can for the cup. Place the cup in the center of a circle on the floor or ground. A player places a playing piece on the edge of the circle and uses the flipper to try to flip the piece into the can. Missing the can means the piece must be flipped from its landing spot. The first player to flip all four pieces into the can wins.

LISTEN! LISTEN! HEAR THAT SOUND?

Medial	Final
anchor	chunk
blanket	drank
cranky	flunk
tanker	sink
Yankee	stink
	trunk

Hummingbird

Quick as a flick
    of a tiddlywink,
she whips in my yard
    for a sip
      of a drink
that's pinker than pink.
    Then zip!
With a flip,
    before I can think,
She's gone in a blink.

Evelyn Amuedo Wade

Final Blends:

n k

nt

Auntie's Elephant

by
Carol A. Losi

TARGETED SOUND

Final blend -**nt** as in **ant:**

auntie's, elephant, auntie, can't, plant

ADDITIONAL SOUND

Short vowel **a** as in **cat:**

auntie, has, an, stamp, can't, flap, grab, plant

 FOCUSING TALK

▪ Talk about "planting" feet firmly on the floor, "planting" a kiss on someone's cheek, or "planting" a surprise.

▪ Talk about homophones and homographs whose different meanings can confuse or entertain us. Examples might include: a *foot* that's used to measure or to walk, *ants* whom we would not want as relatives, *bark* that doesn't make a sound, or a ballroom that has no (sports) balls in it. Children will enjoy your including such words in conversation. For example, you might talk about wanting "pop" (dad or a soda drink?), a plant that needs to "root" (form roots or cheer?), or needing a "slip" to get out of school (paper or underskirt?).

 ACTIVITY: PLANTING ELEPHANTS

Help children draw a zoo scene and a large planter box. Have children cut out or draw pictures of elephants and elephant plants and "plant" each in its appropriate scene. At another time, children will enjoy laying chocolate candy kisses in colored coconut to "plant kisses."

 LISTEN! LISTEN! HEAR THAT SOUND?

Medial	Final
antler	aunt
centipede	event
dental	faint
gently	hint
gigantic	mint
plenty	paint
twenty	print
	splint

Auntie's Elephant

My auntie has an elephant.
It has four feet to stamp, but can't.
It has two ears to flap, but can't.
It has one trunk to grab, but can't.
My auntie has an elephant
but I can't ride it—
It's a plant.

Carol A. Losi

Final Blends:

nt

nt

Please Be Gentle

by
Babs Bell Hajdusiewicz

TARGETED SOUND

Final blend **-nt** as in **ant:** gentle, dentist, giant, complaint, faint

ADDITIONAL SOUNDS

Consonant **j**/soft **g** as in **joy/giant**: gentle, giant

Long vowels: please, be, to, giant, while, I, complaint, I'm, afraid, might, faint

FOCUSING TALK

▪ Try saying, "Please be gentle while *we* check out your complaint," when mediation seems warranted during a dispute. Or say, " 'Please be gentle,' says the student to the teacher" as you recognize a child's hope that you will be gentle. You might also say teasingly, "I'm afraid that you might faint!" to explain reluctance in a particular situation.

▪ Say, "Said the writer to the reader" to comment on an author's intended message. Similarly, you might say, "Said the pitcher to the catcher" when one player appears to be guiding another. Or pretend a task, itself, is speaking to a child: "Said the papers to (child's name)."

ACTIVITY: PLEASE BE GENTLE!

Help children construct a fragile project, such as a tower of blocks or a house made of craft sticks. Invite children to be gentle and prevent destruction as they replace a top block on the tower or add a small object to serve as a chimney. Model use of the poem's words, "Please be gentle!" or innovate to say, "We'll/I'll be gentle," as children watch each other's attempts.

LISTEN! LISTEN! HEAR THAT SOUND?

Medial	Final
acquainted	amount
cents	can't
plentiful	complaint
rented	elephant
splinter	front
	invent
	plant
	pleasant
	punt
	squint
	stunt

Please Be Gentle

"Please be gentle!"
said the dentist to the giant.
"Please be gentle
while I check out your complaint."

"Please be gentle!"
said the giant to the dentist.
"Please be gentle!
I'm afraid that I might faint!"

Babs Bell Hajdusiewicz

Final Blends:

nt

nt

Too Blunt

by
Ellen Raieta

TARGETED SOUND

Final blend **-nt** as in **ant:**

> blunt, flaunting, chants, grant, gently, doesn't, hint, taunted, pants, mint, meant, Runt, sent, pleasant

ADDITIONAL SOUNDS

R-blends:

> grant, pretty, tried, bragging, cruel, friends

FOCUSING TALK

▪ Refer to dull pencils or crayon tips as "blunt" and use the phrases *to put it bluntly* and *I won't be blunt* in response to children's questions. Help children use *blunt* in lieu of *not nice* or *mean.* Use *flaunt* to talk about "showing off" or "bragging" and *taunt* instead of *tease.*

▪ Quote or innovate on the poem's text in appropriate situations. For example, you might say, "You tried to tell me gently, but I didn't take a hint," "I hope that we'll be friends again," "I'm sorry I was blunt," or "She only meant to help you, but she goofed. . . ."

ACTIVITY: MAGNIFICENT PRINTS

Have children use a pencil lead to color over a small area on a sheet of paper. Children can then press a finger on the penciled paper to take a fingerprint. Place cellophane tape over the blackened finger, remove the tape, and stick the "magnificent" fingerprint onto a clean sheet of paper. At another time, provide coins, thin paper, and crayons for children to use in making coin rubbings. Children might fill a whole sheet of paper with coin rubbings to make "magnificent" amounts of money that are "worth a mint."

LISTEN! LISTEN! HEAR THAT SOUND?

Medial		Final	
Atlanta	mints	bent	magnificent
century	printing	chant	present
dainty	recently	count	slant
gentleman		frantic	sprint
		hunt	tint

Too Blunt

Stacie's always flaunting things.
    She chants, "Hey, look at *this!*"
I'll grant her stuff is pretty cool.
    It's also hard to miss.

I've tried to tell her gently,
    but she doesn't take a hint.
So I taunted her for bragging
    that her pants were worth a mint.

I only meant to help her,
    but I goofed and called her "Runt."
Now Stacie's telling everyone
    that I was cruel and blunt.

I hope that we'll be friends again.
    I sent a pleasant letter.
It said, "I'm sorry I was blunt."
    (I hope it makes things better.)

Ellen Raieta

Final Blends:

nt

3-letter Blends

scr as in **scrap**
shr as in **shrub**
spl as in **splash**
spr as in **sprig**
squ as in **squash**
str as in **string**
thr as in **three**

scr

scr
Scroungers

by
Babs Bell Hajdusiewicz

scr

scr

scr

scr

scr

TARGETED SOUND

3-letter blend **scr** as in **scrap:**

scroungers, scramble, scrounge, scrumptious, scrap, screen, screeches, scram

ADDITIONAL SOUND

Short vowel **a** as in **cat:**

scramble, scrap, scram

 ### FOCUSING TALK

▪ Tell children about a scrumptious meal you've prepared or enjoyed. You might also talk about a dog that "scrounged" for food, or comment on a "scrounger scrambling" when you or a child attempts to glean food crumbs during snacktime or lunchtime. Substitute *cupboard door* or *refrigerator door* for *screen door* in the poem to tell a story about someone getting "caught" while scrounging for a midnight snack.

▪ Children will enjoy hearing you describe them as being *scrupulous* when they are honest or conscientious. Ask children to *scrutinize* their work to be sure they've done what was required or *scrutinize* a work area to be sure it is well tidied.

 ### ACTIVITY: SCRATCHY SCRAPERS

Provide nylon net and rubber bands for children to use in making pot scrubbers for use at home. Help children cut the net into 1-inch by 5-inch strips, form a pile of strips, and loop a rubber band around the middle until the strips are tightly secured.

 ### LISTEN! LISTEN! HEAR THAT SOUND?

Initial		**Medial**
Scrabble	scroll	inscribe
scraggly	Scrooge	subscription
scratchy	scrub	
scrawny	scruffy	
scream	scrunch	
screen	scrupulous	
scribble	scrutinize	

Scroungers

Scroungers
scramble
to scrounge up
every scrumptious scrap—
until the screen door screeches.
Then they scram!

Babs Bell Hajdusiewicz

scr

Skyscraper

by
Babs Bell Hajdusiewicz

TARGETED SOUND

3-letter blend **scr** as in **scrap:**

skyscraper, scraping, scream, skyscraping, scratch, scrape

ADDITIONAL SOUNDS

Long vowel **a** as in **ate:**

skyscraper, scraping, making, skyscraping, scrape, make

Consonant **y** as **i** as in **sky:**

skyscraper, why, sky, sky's, cry, skyscraping

FOCUSING TALK

▪ Quote the poem whenever stormy clouds threaten rain, or when there's discussion about skyscrapers or a new skyscraper under construction in your area.

▪ Innovate on the poem's words to encourage children's careful handling of materials. For example, when someone handles a computer disk or a CD carelessly, you might say, "Be kind to the disk. Don't scratch it. Don't scrape it. Don't make the disk cry."

ACTIVITY: A SKYSCRAPER

Help children tear out eight magazine pages and roll each page side to side to make tall tight rolls. Stand the rolls together in a closed circle and secure with tape. Cut a large circle from a magazine cover or heavy paper, slit the circle from the outer edge to the center, and overlap the cut edges to make a cone. Tape or glue the cone over the top of the paper tube rolls.

LISTEN! LISTEN! HEAR THAT SOUND?

Initial		Medial
scram	scrawl	inscription
scrambled	screw	unscramble
scrambler	scribe	
scrapbook	scrimmage	
scrape	script	
scrappy	Scripture	
scratch		

Skyscraper

Skyscraper, why
are you scraping the sky?
The sky's gonna scream.
The sky's gonna cry.

Skyscraper, look!
The sky's making tears!
Your skyscraping corners
are skyscraping spears.

Skyscraper, please
be kind to the sky.
Don't scratch it.
Don't scrape it.
Don't make the sky cry.

Babs Bell Hajdusiewicz

3-Letter Blends:

scr

shr

shr

Shrimply Delightful

by
Bonnie Kerr Morris

shr

shr

shr

shr

shr

TARGETED SOUND

3-letter blend **shr** as in **shrub:**

> shrimply, he-shrimp, shrank, shrubs, shrieked, shrillness, shrug, shrewd, shrimp, shredded

ADDITIONAL SOUNDS

Endings:

> better, shrieked, spying, sighed, eyed, planned, wedding, tossed, shredded, couple

Long vowels:

> shrimply, delightful, he-shrimp, behind, sea, lady, to, see, she, shrieked, you, spying, me, he, timidly, I'm, sighed, although, too, shy, eyed, suitor, they, fine, no, rice, threw, seashells

Suffixes:

> shrimply, delightful, timidly, shrillness

FOCUSING TALK

■ When you make an error and need to apologize, shrug as you play on the poem's language to say, "'I'm sorry,' he sighed with a shrug." Similarly, tease children as you quote the poem to say, "You are spying on me!"

■ Tell children they are "shrimply delightful" and that you're *not* too shy to ask for a hug.

ACTIVITY: SHRIMPLY DELIGHTFUL

Have children draw or copy, enlarge, and cut out pictures of two shrimp. Provide fabric scraps for children to use in "dressing up" the shrimp for their wedding. Children might add underwater shrubs, along with real macaroni shells or pieces of seashells.

LISTEN! LISTEN! HEAR THAT SOUND?

Initial
shred
shredding
shrill
shrink
shrunk

Shrimply Delightful

A he-shrimp once shrank behind sea shrubs,
His lady love better to see,
She shrieked in alarm when she saw him
And said, "You are spying on me!"

He timidly shrank from her shrillness.
"I'm sorry," he sighed with a shrug.
"Although you are shrimply delightful,
I'm too shy to ask for a hug."

That shrewd lady shrimp eyed her suitor.
They planned a fine wedding with bells.
The guests tossed no rice on the couple.
Instead, they threw shredded seashells.

Bonnie Kerr Morris

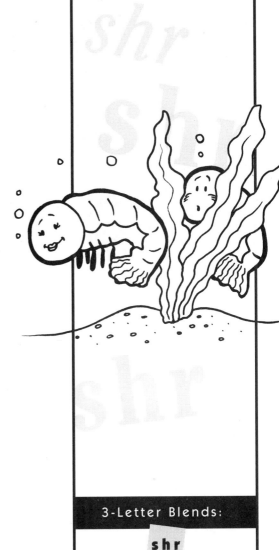

3-Letter Blends:

shr

shr

shr

SHRIE-E-EK!

by
Babs Bell Hajdusiewicz

shr

shr

shr

shr

TARGETED SOUND

3-letter blend **shr** as in **shrub:**

> shrie-e-ek, shriek, shrike, shrub, shrew's

ADDITIONAL SOUNDS

Consonant **k**/hard **c** as in **kite/cat:**

> shrie-e-ek, shriek, shrike, seeking

Short vowels:

> it's, of, in, shrub, when, grub

FOCUSING TALK

▪ Quote the poem's words "Hear the shriek? It's the song . . ." to encourage children to identify any odd sound they hear.

▪ Innovate on the poem's words to comment on someone's eagerness to eat lunch or a snack: "There's a (boy/girl/animal) seeking grub."

ACTIVITY: SHRINKING SQUARES

Provide small squares of unbleached muslin or cotton fabric and paper. Have each child lay a fabric square on paper and draw around it to form an outline. Then help children wash the fabric squares in warm water, lay them out to dry, and press with an iron, if needed. Place a fabric square inside its outline to compare the square's size before and after washing. Talk about clothing items that shrink when they are laundered and the advantages and/or disadvantages of shrinkage.

LISTEN! LISTEN! HEAR THAT SOUND?

Initial
shrank
shrieking
shrimp
shrimpy
shrug

SHRIE–E–EK!

Hear the shriek?
It's the song
of a shrike
in a shrub.
It's the shriek
of a shrike
when a shrew's
seeking grub.
SHRIE-E-EK!

Babs Bell Hajdusiewicz

spl

Splish Splash Rain

by
Marcia Swerdlow

spl

spl

spl

spl

spl

spl

TARGETED SOUND

3-letter blend **spl** as in **splash:**

splish, splash, splashing, sploshing, splooshing, splishing, splattering, spluttering

ADDITIONAL SOUNDS

Ending **-ing** as in **going:**

splashing, sploshing, splooshing, splishing, splattering, spluttering

Short vowels:

splish, splash, splashing, onto, sploshing, under, splishing, from, splattering, on, windows, spluttering, springs, listen, it, sings

 ### FOCUSING TALK

▪ Innovate on the text as needed to talk about paint or mud or milk that splishes and splashes everywhere.

▪ You'll want to recite this poem during a rainstorm, encouraging children to join in.

 ### ACTIVITY: SPLISH! SPLASH!

Take children outside to enjoy this activity. Provide a tape recorder with microphone, and spray-type containers or sprinkling cans filled with water. If possible, include a water hose with sprayer. Help children record the sounds made when they spray water onto different surfaces, such as metal, hard plastic, soft plastic, cardboard, concrete, wood, brick, etc. Encourage children to see how many different sounds they can produce using one type of sprayer. Keep a written record of how each sound was made, for verification later when children listen to and try to identify how they made each sound.

 ### LISTEN! LISTEN! HEAR THAT SOUND?

Initial
splashy
spleen
splendid
split
splotchy
splurge

Splish Splash Rain

Splashing onto sidewalks.
Sploshing under cars.
Splooshing over streetlights.
Splishing from the stars.
Splattering on the windows.
Spluttering over springs.
Listen to the
    splishing
    splashing
    sploshing
      song it sings!

Marcia Swerdlow

3-Letter Blends:

spl

spl

spl

A Splurge

by
Babs Bell Hajdusiewicz

spl

spl

spl

spl

spl

TARGETED SOUND

3-letter blend **spl** as in **splash:**

splurge, splished, sploshed, splashed, splurged, splendid, splendidly

ADDITIONAL SOUNDS

Consonant digraph **sh** as in **ship:**

splished, sploshed, splashed, dishes

Ending **-d/-ed** as in **hoped/waited:**

splished, sploshed, splashed, splurged

Short vowels:

splished, and, sploshed, splashed, dishes, get, them, went, splendid, it, did, job, splendidly, glad

FOCUSING TALK

▪ Children will enjoy hearing about a time when *you've* treated yourself by splurging on something. You might add to the drama by innovating on the text to say, "I splurged and splurged and splurged again. . . ." Children will also enjoy a "splurge" themselves when you suggest straying from any usual classroom routine.

▪ Invite children to join you in a "purge splurge" to clean up a messy area.

ACTIVITY: SPLENDID SPLOSHING

Provide fabric scraps, soap powder, marbles, and two plastic containers with tight-fitting lids. Invite children to place two or three marbles in each container, fill the containers $\frac{2}{3}$ full of water, and add a bit of soap powder to one of the containers. Children can use dirt or pencil shavings to slightly soil the fabric scraps. Place the soiled "clothes" in the "washing machine" and shake vigorously. Wring out the excess water and place scraps in the clear water for a "rinse cycle." Wring and hang out to dry.

LISTEN! LISTEN! HEAR THAT SOUND?

Initial

splatter   splint
splendor   splintery
splice

A Splurge

We splished
　　and sploshed
　　　　and splashed our dishes
　　　　　　trying to get them clean.
Today we went
　　and splurged
　　　　and bought
　　　　　　a splendid new machine.
It splished
　　and sploshed
　　　　and splashed the dishes
　　　　　　while we went out to play.
It did the job
　　quite splendidly!
　　　　I'm glad we splurged today!

Babs Bell Hajdusiewicz

3-Letter Blends:

s p l

spr

spr

In
Springtime

by
Carol Murray

spr

spr

spr

spr

spr

TARGETED SOUND

3-letter blend **spr** as in **sprig:**

> springtime, sprinklers, spray, sprigs, sprout, springer, sprains, sprinting, spruce, spreads, springboards, sprightly, sprawling, sprigtails, spryly, sprattle

ADDITIONAL SOUNDS

Long vowels:

> springtime, spray, make, seedlings, sprains, while, spruce, tree, making, sprightly, sprigtails, spryly, through

Short vowel **i** as in **pin:**

> in, springtime, sprinklers, sprigs, springer, his, sprinting, its, spring-boards, sprigtails

FOCUSING TALK

■ Use the words *sprinting, sprawling, sprightly, spryly,* and *sprattle* to describe children's actions. Children may need a picture clue to recognize a springer spaniel.

■ Introduce children to the use of *sprig* to describe a young person. Innovate on the poem's text as children play-act being "sprigs" who "spryly sprattle" through the room.

ACTIVITY: SPRING HAS SPRUNG!

Have children cut out pictures of sprigs, seeds or seed packets, sprinklers, a springer spaniel, frogs, or pictures of other signs of spring. Help children fold a 1-inch by 6-inch strip of paper accordion-style to make a spring to attach behind each picture. Small pictures can be arranged on a large sheet of paper; larger pictures can be arranged on a bulletin board display.

LISTEN! LISTEN! HEAR THAT SOUND?

Initial	Medial
sprain	espresso
sprang	innerspring
spraying	
spreader	
spring	

In Springtime

In springtime, sprinklers spray the sprigs
    and make the seedlings sprout.

The springer spaniel sprains his foot
    while sprinting all about.

The spruce tree spreads its branches,
    making springboards for the frogs.

And sprightly, sprawling sprigtails
    spryly sprattle through the bogs.

Carol Murray

3-Letter Blends:

spr

spr

Sprinkle
Spree

by
Babs Bell Hajdusiewicz

spr

spr

spr

spr

spr

TARGETED SOUND

3-letter blend **spr** as in **sprig:**

> sprinkle, spree, sprinkled, sprayed

ADDITIONAL SOUND

Long vowel **e** as in **me:**

> spree, we, tree, each

FOCUSING TALK

▪ Talk about a time when you enjoyed a shopping spree, reading spree, playing spree, sprinting spree, or other kind of enjoyable activity.

▪ Present different forms of selected *spr* words to describe common objects or actions. For example, a hinge that springs back quickly can be called a "springy spring," a sprayer that works well can be complimented as a "sprayable sprayer," and a child's handspring might be praised as a "springy handspring."

ACTIVITY: WHICH SOIL IS WETTEST?

Help children collect from several locations soil samples, including some sandy soil and some clay soil. Use a rubber band to secure a fabric scrap over the opening of each of two funnels and suspend each funnel over a glass or clear plastic jar. Put an equal amount of each soil type in each funnel. Measure out the same amount of water and pour over the soil in each funnel. Compare the amount of water that soaks through each soil sample, to determine which soil sample holds the most water or is the wettest.

LISTEN! LISTEN! HEAR THAT SOUND?

Initial	Medial
sprayer	bedspread
spread	handsprings
springy	
sprinkle	
sprint	
sprocket	
spry	

Sprinkle Spree

Today we had a sprinkle spree.
We sprinkled water on the tree.
We sprinkled all the flower beds,
    and then . . .
We sprayed each other's heads!

Babs Bell Hajdusiewicz

3-Letter Blends:

spr

squ

Conversations

by
Ellen Raieta

squ

squ

squ

squ

squ

TARGETED SOUND

3-letter blend **squ** as in **squash:**

squeal, squirrels, squid, squirt, squeak, squawk, squirm

ADDITIONAL SOUNDS

Plural **-s/-es/-ies** as in **dogs/boxes/babies:**

conversations, pigs, whales, squirrels, birds, worms

R-controlled vowel **ur** as in **hurt:**

spurt, squirrels, squirt, birds, worms, squirm

FOCUSING TALK

▪ Add phrases to the poem to include other animals and sounds such as "dogs bark," "crows caw," "cows moo," "snakes hiss," "elephants trumpet," "owls screech," etc. You might also focus on other ways people converse, such as "babies babble," "carolers carol," "speakers speak," or "whisperers whisper."

▪ Use metaphors, such as "she's a mouse," "the chattering squirrels are making a plan right now," or "what a squirmy worm," to describe children's actions.

ACTIVITY: KAZOOS

Help children make kazoos by punching a small hole in a tissue paper tube and securing waxed paper over one end of the tube with a rubber band. Children can put their mouths over the open end of the kazoo and hum or make other noises. Encourage children to make kazoos in different lengths and compare their sounds.

LISTEN! LISTEN! HEAR THAT SOUND?

Initial

squabble

squad

squadron

squall

squander

square

squashy

squeaky

squeegee

Conversations

Pigs squeal.
Whales spurt.
Squirrels chatter.
Squid squirt.
Mice squeak.
Birds squawk.
Worms squirm.
People talk.

Ellen Raieta

squ

squ
Quarrelsome Squirrels

by
Karyn Mazo

squ

squ

squ

squ

squ

TARGETED SOUND

3-letter blend **squ** as in **squash:**

> squirrels, squibble, squabble, squibbling, squabbling, squabbles, squat, squinting, squirm, squanderous, squalor

ADDITIONAL SOUNDS

Consonant **qu** as in **quit:**

> quarrelsome, quibble, quabble, quibbling, quabbling, quietly, quit, tranquility, quiver

Short vowel **i** as in **pin:**

> quibble, squibble, in, quibbling, squibbling, quit, squinting, tranquility, till, quiver, twigs

FOCUSING TALK

▪ Children will enjoy hearing you use *quibble* and *squabble* along with the coined words *quabble* and *squibble* to comment on a disagreement. To introduce *squ* words that may be unfamiliar to children, you might talk about feeling "squeamish" around snakes or mice or another animal you'd rather not touch, or suggest that a child "squelch" a bothersome noise.

▪ The words *tranquility, squanderous, squalor,* and *debris* may be new for children. Look for appropriate times to quote the poem's text to say, "I love the peace and tranquility!" Comment on the "debris" of litter around a trash can, the "squalor" that occurs in the bathroom when people don't flush toilets or leave trash on the floor, or how breaking a crayon or pencil is "squanderous."

ACTIVITY: SQUIGGLY SQUIRMIES

Have children work in pairs to cut several yarn pieces 6 inches in length. One child lays out a number of squiggly yarn lengths so that they're mixed up or slightly intertwined like snakes. As the child points to the "head" of a "squiggly squirmy," the other child must, without moving the pieces, find its "tail." Reverse roles.

LISTEN! LISTEN! HEAR THAT SOUND?

Initial

squaw	squeamish	squirm
squawk	squelch	squirt
squeak	squid	
squeal	squiggle	

Quarrelsome Squirrels

They quibble and quabble
and squibble and squabble
high in the tree above me.

"Excuse me,
Squirrels in the tree,
Could your quibbling and quabbling
and squibbling and squabbling
be done more quietly?"

Surprisingly, they seem to agree.

They quit their squabbles
and squat up there
squinting down at me.

I love the peace and tranquility!

Till suddenly,
their bushy tails
squirm and quiver
and twigs
and nuts
and a squanderous squalor of tree debris
are heaved upon me.

Karyn Mazo

3-Letter Blends:

squ

str

str

Striped Straps

by
Bonnie Compton Hanson

str

str

str

str

str

TARGETED SOUND

3-letter blend **str** as in **string:**

striped, straps, straight, stripped, strong, strips, stray, strip, stripes, string, strange, striped

ADDITIONAL SOUNDS

Long vowel **a** as in **ate:**

straight, stay, fray, stray, strange

Short vowel **i** as in **pin:**

will, stripped, with, strips, if, strip, string, thing

FOCUSING TALK

▪ Children will enjoy hearing your tongue get twisted as you try to say this poem several times in a row. On another occasion, talk about the similar meanings and usage of the words *strips* and *stripes*. Then interchange the poem's words *stripped, strip,* and *strips* with *striped, stripes,* and *stripped,* in that order.

▪ Refer to stripes as "tiger stripes" or "zebra stripes." Challenge children to notice the striped effect visible in many objects, such as woven or knitted cuffs on a sweater or shirt, tops of socks, treads on soles of many types of gym shoes, hardwood boards on a gymnasium floor, tiles and metal frames in suspended ceilings, lined paper, etc.

ACTIVITY: STRIPS AND STRIPES

Provide 1-inch by 11-inch strips of colored paper. Show children how to weave the strips to make a woven mat or pad. At other times, children might arrange strips to form a "cage" effect over a pictured animal, or transform a plain paper bag into a striped bag. Children will also enjoy drawing lines on either side of a ruler to turn plain paper into striped paper.

LISTEN! LISTEN! HEAR THAT SOUND?

Initial
strange
strangely
strawberry
stray

Striped Straps

Will straight straps stripped
With strong strips stay?
Or might those stripped straps
Fray and stray?
If I strip straps
With stripes and string,
What might I call
My strange striped thing?

Bonnie Compton Hanson

str

str
Old Stravinsky

by
Carol Murray

str
str
str
str
str

TARGETED SOUND

3-letter blend **str** as in **string:**

Stravinsky, stricken, stretcher, stretched, strength, stripped, strung, stress, strenuous, struggles, string, stroked, strands

ADDITIONAL SOUNDS

Short vowel **e** as in **red:**

Professor, stretcher, stretched, strength, stress, strenuous, left, mess, fed

Short vowel **i** as in **pin:**

Stravinsky, stricken, with, in, him, his, stripped, string

FOCUSING TALK

▪ Talk about a time when you or someone you know was "strung out with stress" and how you or the person worked toward relieving the stress. At another time, innovate on the poem's words as you stroke strands of your hair, or talk about showing someone "that all of us care." You'll want to tell children that gout is a painful disease of the joints, which often involves the big toe.

▪ When appropriate, quote the poem's lines, "His strength had been stripped," or "his strenuous struggles," to comment on a child's physical activities.

ACTIVITY: STRETCHERS

Provide toothpicks and fabric scraps for children to use in constructing tiny stretchers. Children can glue or staple the fabric over the toothpicks, and then transport small toys on their stretchers.

LISTEN! LISTEN! HEAR THAT SOUND?

Initial
straw
stream
strength
stripe
stroll

Old Stravinsky

Professor Stravinsky
    was stricken with gout,
so we hauled in a stretcher
    and stretched him on out.

His strength had been stripped;
    he was strung out with stress,
and his strenuous struggles
    had left him a mess.

So we fed him string beans
    and stroked strands of his hair—
We showed Old Stravinsky
    that all of us care.

Carol Murray

3-Letter Blends:

str

str

str
Strutting to the Banjo Band

by
Dee Lillegard

str

str

str

str

str

TARGETED SOUND

3-letter blend **str** as in **string:**

> strutting, strut, strumming, strummers, strings, strummers', stride, street

ADDITIONAL SOUNDS

Consonant **m** as in **me:**

> strumming, strummers, music, strummers'

Contractions:

> let's, we'll

Short vowel **u** as in **rug:**

> strutting, strut, strumming, strummers, strummers'

FOCUSING TALK

▪ Children will enjoy reciting the poem with you as they move down the hall. Of course, they'll want to substitute *hall* for *street* in the poem's last line.

▪ Use the word *strut* in place of *come, go,* or *walk* as you direct children.

ACTIVITY: STRUMMING PATTERNS

Have children work with partners and strum a pattern for the partner to duplicate. Children can strum fingers or pencils across any ribbed or grooved surface, such as a heater grate, a grate made with popsicle sticks, or a door threshold.

LISTEN! LISTEN! HEAR THAT SOUND?

Initial
strain
strangle
strap
strike
strong

Strutting to the Banjo Band

Let's strut to the strumming
of the strummers of the strings.
Let's strut to the strumming of the strings.
We'll strut to the music
of the banjo strummers' strumming.
We'll stride down the street like kings!

Dee Lillegard

3-Letter Blends:

str

thr

thr

My Threadbare Throw Rug

by
Virginia Mueller

thr

thr

thr

thr

thr

TARGETED SOUND

3-letter blend **thr** as in **three:**

threadbare, throw, threw, thrown, through, thrifty, woodthrush, thriving

ADDITIONAL SOUNDS

Long vowels:

my, throw, so, I, threw, thrown, away, I'm, through, gleaned, thriving, I've

R-controlled vowels/vowel digraphs:

threadbare, door, floor, bird, for, heard

FOCUSING TALK

■ Once children understand that a throw rug is a small rug that can be thrown in place, they'll enjoy your humor when you refer to a large rug as a "Not Throw" rug.

■ To model use of some of the poem's less familiar words, refer to a worn sleeve or sock as "threadbare," talk about "gleaning" information from a book, speak of recycling efforts as being "thrifty," or talk about a plant that's "thriving" in a sunbeam.

ACTIVITY: THREADS BE GONE?

Cut small squares of fabric and help children unravel the sides to make decorative coasters. The discarded threads can be put out for birds to use in building their nests. You'll want to talk about how a coaster might be called "threadbare" if a thread is accidentally pulled from the middle of the coaster.

LISTEN! LISTEN! HEAR THAT SOUND?

Initial	Medial
thrash	anthrax
thread	anthropology
threaten	
thresh	
threshold	
thriller	
throughout	

My Threadbare Throw Rug

My throw rug was so threadbare
    I threw it out the door.
So now my throw rug's thrown away,
    instead of on the floor.

I'm through with threadbare throw rugs
    but a thrifty woodthrush bird
Has gleaned my threadbare throw rug
    for a thriving nest, I've heard.

Virginia Mueller

thr

thr

The Third Throw

by
Babs Bell Hajdusiewicz

thr

thr

thr

thr

thr

TARGETED SOUND

3-letter blend **thr** as in **three:**

> throw, threw, three, through, throwing

ADDITIONAL SOUNDS

Long vowels:

> throw, I, threw, my, three, times, through, neighbor's, window, throwing, days

FOCUSING TALK

▪ Children will enjoy hearing you innovate on the poem's last two lines to make them work in other contexts. For example, you might tell of a disastrous cooking experience and end the story with "Now my *cooking* days are through."

▪ Use the word *thrice* in lieu of *three* in conversations with children. Also, you might want to introduce children to the saying "Third time's a charm," which can be motivating to children to continue trying until they meet with success.

ACTIVITY: THROW TOY

Have children thread string or yarn through thread spools or buttons or beads, and tie the ends to make a bracelet twice the size of their wrist. Invite children to have three tries at throwing the bracelet upward and catching it around their wrist. At another time, children might thread wads of tissue paper or newspaper, to make a large throw toy that they can throw up and then run under and catch as a belt or necklace.

LISTEN! LISTEN! HEAR THAT SOUND?

Initial	Medial
thrice	enthrall
thrifty	rethread
thrive	
throat	
throne	
thrush	
thrust	

The Third Throw

I threw my ball
three times
and on
the last throw
it went through
my neighbor's
third-story window—
now my throwing days
are through!

Babs Bell Hajdusiewicz

3-Letter Blends:

thr

Diphthongs

au/aw as in *haul/claw*

oi/oy as in *oil/boy*

ou/ow as in *out/cow*

au/aw

au

Awesome Augie Auk

by
Babs Bell Hajdusiewicz

au

au

aw

au

aw

au

TARGETED SOUND

Diphthong **au/aw** as in **haul/claw:**

awesome, Augie, auk, all, auks, thought, awfully, audience, often, gawk, squawk, saw, haul, caught, auklets, small, taught, dawn, caused, yawn, ought, although, yawns

(See also Vowel *a* as in *ball/ought/claw.*)

ADDITIONAL SOUNDS

Consonant **k**/hard **c** as in **kite/cat:**

auk, auks, gawk, squawk, caught, auklets, crack, caused

Consonant **l** as in **long:**

all, awfully, haul, help, auklets, learn, small, early, told, although, well

FOCUSING TALK

▪ Children will enjoy being referred to as "awesome auklets." A child's yawn might be called "an awfully awesome yawn."

▪ Substitute "August" for "Augie" in the poem and talk about nicknames the children or you may use.

ACTIVITY: AWESOME STRAWS

Use straws to play pickup sticks, or glue straws together to create three-dimensional objects. Or, provide straws and paint so that children can do straw painting: Place a drop of paint on a piece of shiny shelf paper. Have children blow gently through the straw while moving the paper slightly. Repeat with drops of paint in other colors and let dry.

LISTEN! LISTEN! HEAR THAT SOUND?

Initial	Medial	Final
August	crawl	claw
auto	fault	draw
awe	fawn	law
awful	hawk	raw
awkward	lawn	straw
awning	maul	
	pauper	
	shawl	

Awesome Augie Auk

All the auks thought Augie
    was an awfully awesome auk.
When Augie fished, his audience
    would often gawk and squawk:

"Augie, you're an awesome auk!
    We saw that haul you caught!
We wish you'd help our auklets learn.
    Small auklets must be taught!"

So Augie taught the auklets
    to fish at the crack of dawn.
But the awfully early rising time
    caused all the auklets to yawn.

And soon the auks told Augie,
    "We ought to change our wish.
Although you've taught our auklets well,
    They've caught more yawns than fish!"

Babs Bell Hajdusiewicz

Diphthongs:

au/aw

au

Paul Macaw

by
Babs Bell Hajdusiewicz

au

au

aw

au

aw

au

TARGETED SOUND

Diphthong **au/aw** as in **haul/caw:** Paul, macaw, Hawkins', crawled, Hawkins, draw, sprawled, yawned, drawn, claws, gawked, awe, jaws, squawked, paused, awed, somersaulted, caw

(See also Vowel *a* as in *ball/ought/claw.*)

ADDITIONAL SOUNDS

Ending **-d/-ed** as in **hoped/waited:** crawled, sprawled, yawned, watched, gawked, squawked, paused, awed, somersaulted

Long vowels: day, old, to, knee, see, she'd, tree, he, open, beak, too, speak, tail, me

R-blends: crawled, draw, sprawled, across, drawn, tree

FOCUSING TALK

▪ Comment that you "gawked in awe" or felt "too awed to speak" when you observed something that pleased or surprised you.

▪ Extend the poem's drawing. Encourage children to think and talk about what Paul might do or say if Miss Hawkins drew claws on the macaw's wing or a beak on the macaw's feet. Help children tell about their ideas with sentences, such as, "Paul saw a flaw. He saw Miss Hawkins draw. . . ."

ACTIVITY: AWESOME ANIMALS

Invite children to cut out pictures of animals from old magazines. Help children cut each animal picture into pieces to have pieces showing a leg, an eye, a beak, a wing, etc. Have children work in pairs and take turns, with one child assembling an animal picture piece-by-piece until the partner can recognize the animal. Children might then repeat the activity to incorrectly assemble an animal picture. In this case, the partner must recognize any flaws in the picture.

LISTEN! LISTEN! HEAR THAT SOUND?

Initial	Medial	Final
auction	because	flaw
auditorium	laundry	jaw
Australia	lawyer	paw
author	sausage	saw
autograph	taut	thaw
automatic		

Paul Macaw

One day, Miss Hawkins' old macaw
    crawled up to watch Miss Hawkins draw.
Paul sprawled across Miss Hawkins' knee,
    then yawned to see she'd drawn a tree.

He watched Miss Hawkins draw some claws—
    Paul gawked in awe, with open jaws.
He watched her draw a head . . . a beak—
    Paul squawked, then paused—too awed to speak.

He watched her draw a tail . . . a wing!
    Now Paul Macaw began to sing!
He somersaulted off her knee.
    "Caw! Caw!" he squawked.
"Old Paul! That's ME!"

Babs Bell Hajdusiewicz

Diphthongs:

au/aw

oi

His Foibles

by
Dee Lillegard

oi

oy

oi

oy

oi

TARGETED SOUND

Diphthong **oi/oy** as in **oil/boy:**

foibles, boisterous, noisy, choice, spoiled, annoying, voice, turmoil, avoid boiling, loyal, joyful

 ## FOCUSING TALK

▪ Children will enjoy hearing about the best dog you or a friend has had. You may also want to use the words *foibles, boisterous,* and *turmoil* to describe your own or a friend's trying experience with a pet.

▪ Tell children about a loyal friend or pet you've known and the behaviors they exhibited that showed loyalty. As you point out children's loyal behaviors, whether toward you or their peers, talk about how loyal behaviors affect others' feelings.

 ## ACTIVITY: FIRST CHOICES

Provide copies of pictures of all kinds of dogs so that each child can select a "first choice" for a pet. Encourage children to give reasons for their choices. To display children's pet choices, you might post a pet picture alongside a speech bubble. For example, a collie might be "saying," "I am Joyce's first choice because I have long hair."

 ## LISTEN! LISTEN! HEAR THAT SOUND?

Initial	Medial	Final
oily	boil	alloy
oyster	coil	convoy
	embroider	corduroy
	hoist	soy
	loin	Troy
	loiter	

His Foibles

He is boisterous.
He is noisy.
And he wasn't Dad's first choice.
He is spoiled
and it's annoying
when he doesn't heed my voice.

He brings turmoil that I can't avoid.
He makes me boiling mad.
But he's loyal
and he's joyful—
and the best dog I have had.

Dee Lillegard

Diphthongs:

oi/oy

oi/oy

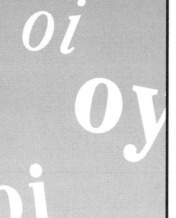

oi
Royal Coils

by
Babs Bell Hajdusiewicz

oi

oy

oi

oy

oi

TARGETED SOUND

Diphthong **oi/oy** as in **oil/boy:**

> royal, coils, Loi, enjoyed, toys, noise, Boink, annoyed, Floyd, noisy, destroyed, destroy, oil, coil, enjoys, Boing

ADDITIONAL SOUND

Consonant **l** as in **long:**

> royal, coils, Loi, liked, all, I'll, oil, coil

FOCUSING TALK

▪ Say, "Boing! Boing!" or "Boink! Boink!" when a strange noise is heard. When appropriate, you might say, "All that noise annoyed (person's name)." You might also use *foiled* to talk about a plan that didn't work.

▪ Children will enjoy your pretending to oil them as you say "I'll fix that noise!" Help children to respond by saying, "Please don't destroy our (descriptive word, such as *giggly* or *wiggly*) noise!"

ACTIVITY: COILED TOYS

Wind a pipe cleaner around a pencil to make a coil. Tape the coil onto a small toy animal or person, or cut out a magazine picture of a person or an animal, and add coils so that the character can do springy "exercises." At another time, cut out a large paper circle or use a lightweight paper plate and make a coiled snake. Cut into the edge of the circle to form a 1-inch strip around the edge; continue cutting a spiral to the center of the circle; shape one end of the spiral to be the snake's head; hang the coiled snake from string. Children might also roll clay into a rope to form a coiled snake.

LISTEN! LISTEN! HEAR THAT SOUND?

Initial	Medial	Final
oink	foil	ahoy
Oilers	join	boy
	loyal	buoy
	moist	toy
	soil	
	toil	
	void	

Royal Coils

Queen Loi enjoyed her royal toys.
She even liked their squeaky noise—
    BOINK! BOINK!
But all the noise annoyed King Floyd.
"Those noisy toys must be destroyed!"

The queen exclaimed, "I'll fix that noise!
You can't destroy my royal toys!"
Queen Loi put tiny drops of oil
on every noisy royal coil.
And now King Floyd tells everyone,
"This BOING! BOING! exercise is fun!"

Babs Bell Hajdusiewicz

Diphthongs:

oi/oy

ou

ou

**Scowling
Owl**

by
Richard Michelson

ou

ow

ou

ow

ou

TARGETED SOUND

Diphthong **ou/ow** as in **out/cow:**

> scowling, owl, prowl, scowl, growl, bow-wow, meow, howl

ADDITIONAL SOUND

Consonant **l** as in **long:**

> scowling, owl, prowl, scowl, always, only, learn, growl, howl

FOCUSING TALK

▪ Innovate on the poem's last line to create "Whoooooo Am I?" riddles. Examples might include a crow that says, "I'm tired of always cawing, 'Caw'," or a hen that says, "I'm tired of always clucking, 'Cluck'." You might also innovate on the poem's first stanza to create a riddle about a bat that "spends nighttimes on the prowl" or a snake that "spends its winters in the ground."

▪ Use the poem's pattern to tell children about things you would like to learn to do. You might say, "If only I could learn to dive, or ski, or. . . ."

ACTIVITY: SCOWLING FACES

Provide paper plates or lids from margarine tubs, rubber bands in various sizes and colors, and glue. Using the plates or lids as faces, children can position and then glue on rubber bands as eyes, eyebrows, noses, mouths, hair, and ears. Encourage children to talk about situations that cause them to scowl as they experiment with different rubber band shapes to make mouths, eyes, and eyebrows that appear to be scowling.

LISTEN! LISTEN! HEAR THAT SOUND?

Initial	Medial	Final
ounce	blouse	allow
ourselves	cloud	cow
out	couch	how
outdoors	flower	now
	house	somehow
	loud	
	mouth	

Scowling Owl

I spend my nighttimes on the prowl
    for rats,
    but that's not why I scowl.
I'm tired of always screeching, "Whooo."

If only I could learn to growl,
    or bow-wow,
    moo,
    meow,
    or howl—
I'm tired of always screeching, "Whooo."

Richard Michelson

Diphthongs:

ou/ow

ou

The Sound of the Wind

by
Christina Rossetti

TARGETED SOUND

Diphthong **ou/ow** as in **out/cow:**

> sound, town, down

ADDITIONAL SOUND

Final blend **-nd** as in **and:**

> sound, wind, windy

FOCUSING TALK

▪ Quote the poem's first two lines on a windy, rainy day. If you are near a lake or an ocean, the poem's third line will be very meaningful to children. Help children recognize that in years gone by, wind and rain often made ships go down. Then check their understanding of those time concepts by asking during a storm, "Will the ships go down?"

▪ Children will enjoy your references to the poem's rhythm and its repetitive question. For example, you might ask, "Will the zipper go down? Will the zipper go down? Oh, will the zipper go down, go down?" In addition, to adding some fun to a situation, you'll find that such a poetic reference can be helpful in easing a child's frustration.

ACTIVITY: RECORDING SOUNDS

Provide a tape recorder for children to use in recording sounds that include the *ou/ow* sound. For example, children will enjoy using different intonations and decibel levels to say "meow," "ouch," or "bow-wow," or to imitate the sound of a dog howling. At other times, model sentences such as the following that children can say and record: "An owl is outside," "I prowl downtown," "I shout in the shower."

LISTEN! LISTEN! HEAR THAT SOUND?

Initial	Medial	Final
outline	around	plow
outside	shout	sow
owl	shower	vow
owlet	sound	
	south	
	towel	
	town	
	trout	

The Sound of the Wind

The wind has such a rainy sound
Moaning through the town,
The sea has such a windy sound—
Will the ships go down?

The apples in the orchard
Tumble from their tree—
Oh will the ships go down, go down,
On the windy sea?

Christina Rossetti

Diphthongs:

ou/ow

ou

Under the Ground

by
Babs Bell Hajdusiewicz

ou

ow

ou

ow

ou

TARGETED SOUND

Diphthong **ou/ow** as in **out/cow:**

ground, down, sound, underground

ADDITIONAL SOUNDS

Final blend **-nd** as in **and:**

under, ground, sound, underground

Long vowel **u** as in **pool:**

whoosh-a, zoom, zooming, through, room

FOCUSING TALK

▪ As befits a situation, substitute another word in the poem for *ground*. For example, children may be huddling under a *roof* for shelter or playing under a *slide*. Talk about other things that move under the ground.

▪ The cause of any unidentified sound might be questioned using the poem's words "Rumble, rumble, rumble, rumble, what's that sound?" Using the same phrase pattern, try substituting words for *rumble,* such as *crinkle, gurgle,* or *bubble.*

ACTIVITY: AN UNDERGROUND VIEW

Help children draw or use cut paper to create a mural showing such underground things as a subway tunnel, a large tree's roots, a mole or snake hole, grass roots, and tunnels made by worms.

LISTEN! LISTEN! HEAR THAT SOUND?

Initial	Medial	Final
ouch	about	bow
outfield	around	eyebrow
outlandish	count	snowplow
outstanding	doubt	
	fowl	
	gown	
	mountain	
	powder	

Under the Ground

Down
Down
Down
Down
Under the ground.
Rumble
Rumble
Rumble
Rumble
What's that sound?
Whoosh-a
Rumble
Whoosh-a
Rumble
Zoom
Zoom
Zoom
The subway train is zooming
through its underground room.

Babs Bell Hajdusiewicz

Diphthongs:

ou/ow

Word Endings

-d/-ed as in ***hoped/waited***

-er as in ***darker***

-est as in ***softest***

-ing as in ***going***

-le as in ***table***

d/ed

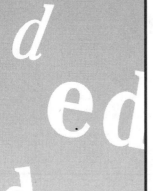

ed

I Did It!

by
Babs Bell Hajdusiewicz

d

ed

ed

d

ed

TARGETED SOUND

Ending **-d/-ed** as in **hoped/waited:**

tried, cried

ADDITIONAL SOUNDS

Consonant **d** as in **dad:**

did, tried, cried

Long vowel **i** as in **like:**

I, tried, cried

FOCUSING TALK

▪ You'll find this poem helpful when you or a child is feeling frustrated while trying to do a task. At times, you may want to use only the first or last portion of the poem, or reverse the poem's order to say, "I cried and cried . . . and then I tried . . . *and* I did it."

▪ Tell children about a time when you experienced feelings expressed in the poem. Children familiar with the poem will appreciate your parodies or humorous innovations. For example, you might say, ". . . cried and cried and then I quit . . . *and* dried my tears." Similarly, you might substitute other verbs to create funny versions, and say "I poured and poured and poured and poured and then I quit *and* spilled."

ACTIVITY: MIRRORED IMAGES

Children will be eager to keep trying until they meet with success at these three activities using mirrors: 1. Position a mirror such that an object in another part of a room is reflected in the mirror. 2. Hold a mirror and stand with your back to another mirror so that you see your back and your left or right profile. 3. Place paper and pen or pencil in front of a stand-up mirror and show children how to write on the paper so that a (reversed) letter or number appears correctly written in the mirror.

LISTEN! LISTEN! HEAR THAT SOUND?

Final

closed	hoped	surfed
cooked	mowed	vacuumed
glued	opened	
helped	poured	

I Did It!

I tried
and tried
and tried
and tried
and then I quit
and cried.
I cried
and cried
and cried
and cried
and then I quit
and tried
and
I did it!

Babs Bell Hajdusiewicz

d/ed

ed

She Begged and Pleaded

by
Babs Bell Hajdusiewicz

TARGETED SOUND

Ending **-d/-ed** as in **hoped/waited:**

> begged, pleaded, asked, mixed, stirred, poured, added, spilled, handed, dropped, promised, sighed

ADDITIONAL SOUNDS

Short vowel **a** as in **cat:**

> and, asked, Daddy, added, handed, stand, can

Short vowel **i** as in **pin:**

> Sissy, mixed, spilled, it, promised, still, in, spill

FOCUSING TALK

- Tell children a personal story that includes verbs with the inflectional *-ed* ending. For example, you might say, "I *wanted* a piece of candy, so I *hunted* and *hunted* and was feeling *frustrated* until my friend *handed* me just what I *wanted*."

- Tell children about a time when you *listed* things you *needed* to do and then *crossed* off each task as you *completed* it. For instance, you might say, "I *needed* to mow the lawn. I *mowed* the lawn and then *crossed* it off my list."

ACTIVITY: SPILLED AND ADMIRED

Provide glue, heavy paper, and objects, such as rice, beans, or seeds. Have children spill some glue onto the paper and spread it around. Then have children spill the objects onto the paper, press them into the glue, and let dry. Ask children to study their spilled art to identify any recognizable shapes or designs.

LISTEN! LISTEN! HEAR THAT SOUND?

Final

added	mopped	started
dated	nodded	subtracted
finished	parted	trotted
jogged	pasted	twisted
kissed	regarded	typed
listed	rooted	wished
looked		

She Begged and Pleaded

Sissy asked for lemonade,
    so Daddy mixed some up.
He stirred and poured and added ice.
    Then Sissy spilled the cup.

Sissy begged for lemonade,
    so Daddy poured some more.
He handed her a fresh cup full.
    She dropped it on the floor.

Sissy pleaded for lemonade.
    She promised she'd stand still.
But Daddy put her in the tub,
    And sighed, "*Now,* you can spill."

Babs Bell Hajdusiewicz

Word Endings:

d/ed

er

A Slicker Quicker Ride

by
Carol Murray

TARGETED SOUND

Ending **-er** as in **darker:** slicker, quicker, smoother, faster, longer, high-er, brisker, swifter, steeper, stronger, sleeker

ADDITIONAL SOUNDS

Blends: slicker, smoother, faster, longer, brisker, swifter, steeper, stronger, sleeker, slippery, slide

Long vowels: ride, I, smoother, higher, steeper, sleeker, slide

Short vowels: slicker, quicker, faster, brisker, swifter, on, slippery

FOCUSING TALK

- Talk about how a sticky spot on a slide makes the ride bumpy and not as much fun. Then ask children to listen carefully as you read the poem and add or substitute other comparison words ending in -er. You might have children say "bump!" when they hear a comparison word such as *slower* that doesn't go with the other words or doesn't make sense in the context of a fun slide down a tall, slippery slide. Try using words such as *scarier, lower, bumpier, shorter,* or *weaker.*

- Innovate on the text by reading the poem backwards as if you were slowly climbing up a slide for another turn. You might say, "I took a slippery, quicker, . . . climb up a . . . smoother slide." At another time, innovate on the text to tell about going up a tall, scary ladder.

ACTIVITY: WHICH IS SMOOTHER?

Provide course, medium, and fine grades of sandpaper, along with unfinished scraps of wood. Invite children to choose two different grades of sandpaper and predict which grade will produce a smoother effect on the wood surface. Have children then check their predictions by sanding the wood in two places, using two different grades of sandpaper.

LISTEN! LISTEN! HEAR THAT SOUND?

Final

angrier	lower
colder	taller
dirtier	thinner
happier	warmer
healthier	weaker

A Slicker Quicker Ride

I took a
   smoother
      faster
        longer
          higher
            brisker
              swifter
              ride
                on a
                  steeper
                    stronger
                    sleeker
                      slicker
                        quicker
                          slippery slide.

Carol Murray

Word Endings:

er

er

er

A Newer Me

by
Babs Bell Hajdusiewicz

TARGETED SOUND

Ending **-er** as in **darker:**

newer, bigger, taller, older, stronger

ADDITIONAL SOUNDS

Consonant **l** as in **long:**

taller, older, I'll, school, fall

Long vowels:

newer, me, older, I'll, be, I, to, school

FOCUSING TALK

▪ Innovate on the poem's words to describe other ideas, such as "A Warmer Me": Warmer/Dryer/Cleaner/Safer/That is what I'll be/When I put on my winter clothes/I'll be a warmer Me. Encourage children to help create other versions, such as "A Kinder Me," "A Quieter Me," or "A Healthier Me."

▪ Call upon the poem's ideas and rhythm before an activity, such as lunch or recess, to say, "When I come back from lunch today, I'll be a fuller Me" or "When I come back from recess time, I'll be a fresher Me."

ACTIVITY: A NEWER ME

Have children work in pairs to draw outlines of their bodies onto large sheets of paper. Then have children draw a second outline one inch or so outside the first outline to show possible growth over a summer. Help children cut out their body shapes on the second or outside line. Children might color the space between the two lines. Children who will return to the school in the fall will enjoy viewing their "Newer Me" shapes on a hallway wall. Children might then want to repeat the activity to compare their predicted growth to their actual growth.

LISTEN! LISTEN! HEAR THAT SOUND?

Final
busier
cleaner
darker
later
lighter
louder

A Newer Me

Bigger.
Taller.
Older.
Stronger.
That is what I'll be!
When I come back to school next fall,
I'll be a newer Me!

Babs Bell Hajdusiewicz

Word Endings:

er

er

er
When It Comes to Bugs

by
Aileen Fisher

TARGETED SOUND

Ending **-er** as in **darker:** crawlers, creepers, hoppers, jumpers, fliers, leapers, walkers, stalkers, chirpers, peepers, finders, keepers

ADDITIONAL SOUNDS

Long vowel **e** as in **me:** creepers, leapers, peepers, be, keepers

Long vowel **i** as in **like:** I, like, fliers, why, my, finders

Plural **-s/-es/-ies** as in **dogs/boxes/babies:** bugs, crawlers, creepers, hoppers, jumpers, fliers, leapers, walkers, stalkers, chirpers, peepers, finders, keepers

FOCUSING TALK

■ Innovate on the poem's text and rhythm to create a new poem titled "When It Comes to Kids" that might go this way: "I like smilers, I like frowners, workers, players, talkers, clowners, gigglers, wigglers, weepers, peepers. . . . All *my* kids are finders keepers." At other times, try out other ideas, such as "When It Comes to Books," "When It Comes to Pets," or "When It Comes to Parents."

■ Use the phrase "finders keepers" as children pick up things that belong to them. You might make a point about tidying up by asking, "finders keepers?" as you pick up a child's possession that's been carelessly left out.

ACTIVITY: MY BOOK OF . . .

Have children cut out pictures that depict an interesting category word ending in *-er*. Examples might include *runners* for pictures of athletes running, *workers* for pictures of people at work in various jobs, *crawlers* for pictures of bugs, or *timers* for pictures of all sorts of clocks. Staple sheets of paper together to make a book for each child's collection. Help children title their books using the category word ending in *-er*.

LISTEN! LISTEN! HEAR THAT SOUND?

Final

brighter	lonlier
eater	loser
folder	planter
helper	safer
hitter	skater
leader	winner

When It Comes to Bugs

I like crawlers,
I like creepers,
hoppers, jumpers,
fliers, leapers,
walkers, stalkers,
chirpers, peepers . . .

I wonder why
my mother thinks
that finders can't be keepers?

Aileen Fisher

Word Endings:

er

est

est Who's First?

by
Carol A. Losi

TARGETED SOUND

Ending **-est** as in **softest:**

oldest, tallest, boldest, smallest, loudest

ADDITIONAL SOUNDS

Consonant **l** as in **long:**

let's, oldest, tallest, boldest, smallest, loudest

Contractions:

who's, let's

FOCUSING TALK

▪ Quote the poem whenever children are deciding who will be first or last to do an activity. You might want to change the adjective in the poem's last line to encourage or reward a particular behavior.

▪ Substitute other comparison words in the poem. Examples might include *shortest, earliest, latest, youngest, softest, shyest, noisiest, sharpest, dullest, ripest, fastest,* or *slowest.*

ACTIVITY: WHO'S FIRST?

Act out a "Who's First?" game. Ask four children to join you to form a line. Ask who is first, second, third, fourth, and fifth or last. Have everyone turn around to face the opposite direction. Ask who is now first, second, third, fourth, and fifth or last. Which people's numbers change? Which stay the same? At another time, repeat the activity with other numbers of children to explore how the middle person's number always stays the same when the line has an odd number of people.

LISTEN! LISTEN! HEAR THAT SOUND?

Final
brightest
healthiest
kindest
quietest
ripest
roundest

Who's First?

Let's not go by
who's the oldest
or the tallest
or the boldest
or the smallest.
Let's just go by who's the LOUDest.

Carol A. Losi

est

The Littlest Fish

by
Bonnie Kerr Morris

est
est
est
est
est

TARGETED SOUND

Ending **-est** as in **softest:**

> littlest, bluest, saddest, greenest, brightest, sharpest, tiniest

ADDITIONAL SOUNDS

Blends:

> bluest, greenest, brightest, prize, smaller

Consonant digraphs:

> the, fish, teeth, sharpest, should, there's

Consonant **s** as in **so/city:**

> sea, saddest, sigh, see, said

FOCUSING TALK

■ Innovate on the poem's text as appropriate to tell children about a personal experience. For instance, you might tell about a time when you said, "I'm not a big winner. There's no pizza left to be my dinner."

■ Modify the poem's first stanza to tell about a *happy* observation. Change *saddest* to *gladdest,* and invite children to help complete a tale about a fish who sighs a *glad* sigh.

ACTIVITY: COMPARISONS

Provide plastic tubs, tin cans, and cardboard tubes from paper towels and tissue paper cut into varying lengths. Have children sort like objects together and then identify within each group the shortest, longest, tallest, thinnest, deepest, clearest, darkest, lightest, etc.

LISTEN! LISTEN! HEAR THAT SOUND?

Final
fastest
freshest
happiest
hardest
prettiest

The Littlest Fish

The littlest fish
    In the bluest sea
Gave the saddest sigh,
    "I see!" said he.

"I've the greenest tail,
    and the brightest eyes.
My teeth are the sharpest.
    I should get a prize.

But I'm also the tiniest
    and not a big winner—
There's nobody smaller
    To be my dinner."

Bonnie Kerr Morris

Word Endings:

est

est

Bears

by
Carol Murray

est

est

est

est

TARGETED SOUND

Ending **-est** as in **softest:**

scariest, hairiest, blackest, pickiest, trickiest, sweetest

ADDITIONAL SOUNDS

Blends:

Grizzly, scariest, Sloth, Black, blackest, small, Bruin, trickiest, and, sweetest

R-controlled vowel digraphs:

bears, scariest, bear, hairiest

 FOCUSING TALK

▪ Innovate on the poem's words to compare other groups of animals, such as dogs or cats or farm animals. Children will especially enjoy your using this format to favorably compare your own dog or cat to all kinds of dogs or cats.

▪ At Halloween time, you might substitute dressed-up characters' names in the poem. At another time, change the *-est* words to favorably compare your class to past groups you've had or to other classes in the school.

 ACTIVITY: THE SWEETEST BEAR

Invite children to bring in teddy bears for a display of "The Sweetest Bear." Include some candy bears in the display and talk about how, in this case, *sweetest* can suggest *most loveable* or *filled with sugar.*

 LISTEN! LISTEN! HEAR THAT SOUND?

Final
clearest
lightest
longest
sharpest
softest
tallest

Bears

The Grizzly is the scariest.
The Sloth bear is the hairiest.
The Black, no doubt, the blackest, large or small.
Koala is the pickiest.
Old Bruin is the trickiest . . .
And Teddy is the sweetest bear of all.

Carol Murray

ing

Can't Sleep

by
Betsy R. Rosenthal

TARGETED SOUND

Ending **-ing** as in **going:**

tapping, flapping, leaking, creaking, clicking, ticking, pinging, singing

ADDITIONAL SOUNDS

Plural **-s/-es/-ies** as in **dogs/boxes/babies:**

branches, blinds, faucets, floors, dishes, clocks, pipes

FOCUSING TALK

- Substitute other "noisy" night sounds in the poem. Examples might include "dogs barking," "fans whirring," "bells ringing," "rain splashing," etc. At another time, change the poem's verbs and gerunds to past tense to tell about a time when you couldn't sleep: "Couldn't sleep. Branches tapped . . . Blinds flapped . . . House was singing."

- Talk about ways you've found to help yourself get to sleep. Examples might include thinking of fun things you did during the day or will do the next day; repeating a message to yourself, such as "I *will* go to sleep"; or innovating on the counting sheep idea by making a mental list of any number of things that interest you.

ACTIVITY: THINKING ABOUT SLEEPING

Provide string and various kinds of beads and buttons. Have children think about fun things they have done or would like to do and then select a bead or button that can represent that experience. String the beads and buttons and tie the ends together. Encourage children to keep their "Thinking About Sleeping" chains beside their beds to think about, look at, or manipulate as they're trying to sleep.

LISTEN! LISTEN! HEAR THAT SOUND?

Final

cooking	sitting
eating	skiing
meeting	sliding
opening	warning
playing	writing
scaring	

Can't Sleep

Can't sleep.
Branches tapping.
Can't sleep.
Blinds are flapping.
Can't sleep.
Faucets leaking.
Can't sleep.
Floors are creaking.
Can't sleep.
Dishes clicking.
Can't sleep.
Clocks are ticking.
Can't sleep.
Pipes are pinging.
Can't sleep.
House is singing!

Betsy R. Rosenthal

Word Endings:

ing

ing

Monday Morning

by
John C. Head

ing

ing

ing

ing

ing

ing

TARGETED SOUND

Ending **-ing** as in **going:**

morning, moaning, groaning, mumbling, grumbling, glowering, showering, rubbing, scrubbing, washing, sploshing, groping, soaping, howling, toweling, splashing, dashing, muttering, buttering, crunching, munching, sighing, tying, brushing, rushing, cramming, slamming

ADDITIONAL SOUNDS

Blends:

Monday, groaning, mumbling, grumbling, glowering, scrubbing, sploshing, groping, splashing, crunching, brushing, cramming, slamming, and

Consonant digraph **sh** as in **ship:**

showering, washing, sploshing, splashing, dashing, brushing, rushing

FOCUSING TALK

▪ Substitute the names of other days of the week in the poem's title. Add other actions as appropriate to tell about your own preparation for a day at school.

▪ Encourage children's interest in the poem's pattern of rhyming-word pairs by using pairs of rhyming words to talk about various other activities. Examples might include these: "We're fixing and mixing paints," "He's leading the reading," "What a giggling, wiggling group!" Similarly, you might describe a child who's just shared a fact as a "talking walking encyclopedia." Children will be eager to follow your lead as you coin expressions to complete rhyming pairs.

ACTIVITY: RHYMING WORDS

Invite children to choose one of the poem's rhyming-word pairs or create one of their own and then illustrate the two words in a single picture. For example, *brushing* and *rushing* might be illustrated with a dog that's trying to run off while being brushed or with a school bus driver who's honking a horn while a child is anxiously brushing his or her hair.

LISTEN! LISTEN! HEAR THAT SOUND?

Final	doing	
being	helping	tasting
building	sipping	typing
coming	sleeping	watching

Monday Morning

Moaning, groaning,
mumbling, grumbling,
glowering, showering,
rubbing, scrubbing,
washing, sploshing,
groping, soaping,
howling, toweling,
splashing, dashing,
muttering, buttering,
crunching, munching,
sighing, tying,
brushing, rushing,
cramming, slamming,
and off to
school.

John C. Head

Word Endings:

ing

ing

Following Rules at School

by
Betsy Franco

ing
ing
ing
ing
ing

TARGETED SOUND

Ending **-ing** as in **going:**

> following, pushing, running, jumping, hogging, wrestling, cutting, pinching, biting, swearing, dancing, standing, acting, sitting, doing, acting

ADDITIONAL SOUNDS

Blends:

> playground, jumping, from, jungle, classroom, and, swearing, desk, standing, slide

Consonant digraphs:

> pushing, the, pinching, shine, what, there's, that's, why, when

FOCUSING TALK

▪ Quoting the first stanzas of this poem can be a gentle and effective way to remind children of rules. You will, of course, want to innovate on the text to address other behaviors.

▪ Innovate on the text to tell about rules that you, yourself, must follow. You might also innovate on the poem's words to talk about rules in other settings, such as in the home, in a house of worship, or in the car.

ACTIVITY: POSTING RULES

Invite children to illustrate each idea in the poem and then post the rebus rules in appropriate places as helpful reminders.

LISTEN! LISTEN! HEAR THAT SOUND?

Final
catching
creating
flipping
folding
lighting
running
sealing
slipping
soaking
thinking
touching

Following Rules at School

No pushing on the playground
    or running in the hall.
No jumping from the jungle gym,
    or hogging of the ball.

No wrestling in the classroom
    or cutting in the line.
No pinching and no biting
    and no swearing, rain or shine.

No dancing on the desk top
    or standing on the slide.
No acting rough at recess,
    or I'm sitting back inside.

No matter what I'm doing,
    there's always some ol' rule.
That's why I feel like acting wild
    when I get out of school.

Betsy Franco

Word Endings:

ing

le

le

A *Gaggle* of Geese

by
Patricia Hooper

le

le

le

le

le

TARGETED SOUND

Ending **-le** as in **table:** gaggle, giggle, waggle, wiggle, straggle, toddle, struggle, waddle, puddle, middle, paddle, dawdles, diddle, squiggle, dabble, jiggle, gabble, topple, fiddles, trouble, ripple, bubble, hobble, unstable, wobble, table

ADDITIONAL SOUNDS

Consonant **b** as in **boy:** dabble, gabble, trouble, bubble, hobble, unstable, wobble, table

Consonant **d** as in **dad:** toddle, waddle, puddle, middle, paddle, dawdles, diddle, dabble, fiddles

Consonant **g** as in **go:** gaggle, geese, giggle, waggle, wiggle, straggle, struggle, squiggle, jiggle, gathers, gabble

Short vowel **i** as in **pin:** in, it's, giggle, wiggle, it, middle, diddle, swims, with, squiggle, drifts, jiggle, fiddles, ripple, will

Short vowel **u** as in **rug:** struggle, puddle, struts, trouble, bubble, unstable

Suffix **-ly** as in **lonely:** partly, surely, completely, rarely

FOCUSING TALK

▪ Use *gaggle* to denote another kind of group: "gaggle of giggles and wiggles," "gaggle of mittens," "gaggle of wonderful ideas."

▪ Innovate on the poem's text to ask, "What's in a *wiggle*?" or "What's in a *puddle?*"

ACTIVITY: WHAT'S IN A GOOGOL?

Tell children that a googol is a very large number that's written with a "1" followed by 100 zeros. It's true! American mathematician Edward Kasner (1878–1955) coined the word for this number. Ask children to help write a googol and make a book that includes pictures of all sorts of things that *might* be in this world a googol years from now. The book might be titled *In Googol Time*.

LISTEN! LISTEN! HEAR THAT SOUND?
Final

couple	little
fiddle	pedal
griddle	peddle
hospital	reliable
kettle	settle

A *Gaggle* of Geese

What's in a gaggle?
It's partly a giggle,
It's kind of a waggle,
It's sort of a wiggle.

It's sometimes a straggle
And always a toddle
And often a struggle
And surely a waddle.

It comes to a puddle
And moves to the middle,
Then pauses to paddle
Or dawdles to diddle.

It swims with a squiggle
And drifts with a dabble,
Or struts with a jiggle
And gathers to gabble.

It threatens to topple
And fiddles with trouble,
Then drifts on a ripple
And blows you a bubble.

It hops with a hobble
Completely unstable,
Yet rarely will wobble
When served at the table.

Patricia Hooper

Word Endings:

le

TARGETED SOUND

Ending -**le** as in **table**:

puzzle, buckle, handle, tickle, candle, rattle, needle, trickle, middle

ADDITIONAL SOUNDS

Contractions:

it's, doesn't, there's

Short vowels:

it's, puzzle, when, buckle, doesn't, handle, tickle, candle, rattle, thread, trickle, of, in, middle, head

FOCUSING TALK

▪ Innovate on the poem's text to include other puzzling ideas. Consider these examples: "when a giggle doesn't quit," "when a clock doesn't tick," "when a backpack doesn't open," or "when a zipper doesn't zip." Help children go beyond the "because it doesn't work" response by talking about the "why" and the "what do I do now?" aspects when something doesn't work the way we expect.

▪ You'll want to quote the poem's last two lines any time you're puzzled about something. In addition, the two lines may be effective, in lieu of a reprimand, when you'd like a child to end an undesirable behavior.

ACTIVITY: IT'S A PUZZLE!

First, have children illustrate puzzling situations they've experienced. Next, have children glue their pictures onto heavy paper and trim the edges. Help children draw lines to indicate any number of puzzle pieces. Before cutting out the pieces, you may want to help children place a sticky dot or small design on each dividing line of the puzzle as an aid in putting the puzzle back together. Encourage children to exchange puzzles with friends.

LISTEN! LISTEN! HEAR THAT SOUND?

Final

able	dabble	Scrabble
battle	metal	stable
bicycle	nickel	table
cable	pickle	

It's a Puzzle!

When a buckle doesn't buckle,
    Or a handle doesn't turn,
Or a tickle doesn't tickle,
    Or a candle doesn't burn,

When a rattle doesn't rattle,
    Or a needle doesn't thread,
There's a trickle of a puzzle
    In the middle of my head.

Babs Bell Hajdusiewicz

Word Endings:

le

Other Vowel Sounds

a as in ***ball/ought/claw***
u as in ***full***
oo as in ***book***
a/e/o as in ***mama/taken/lemon***
y as *e* in ***very***
y as *i* in ***sky***

Rubber Band Ball

by
Sydnie Meltzer Kleinhenz

TARGETED SOUND

Vowel **a** as in **ball/ought/claw:**

ball, all, hall, small, call

(See also Diphthong *au/aw* as in *haul/claw.*)

ADDITIONAL SOUNDS

Consonant **b** as in **boy:**

rubber, band, ball, doorknob, bands, began, bounce

Consonant **l** as in **long:**

ball, little, all, loop, celery, hall, small, school, mall, help, like, call

FOCUSING TALK

▪ Using the poem's rhythm, innovate on the words to comment on how one paper clip, piece of paper, or some other object is "just not enough at all." Similarly, innovate on the poem's last two lines to encourage a child to bounce another kind of ball.

▪ Introduce children to the homograph *ball* with a comment such as this: "I was having a *ball* at the *ball*game last night until I hit the *ball* of my foot and now I have a *ball* of gauze around my foot and shall never be able to dance at the *ball*."

ACTIVITY: BALL OF PEACE

Provide rubber bands and a tennis ball or small rubber ball. Invite children to add a rubber band to the ball each time they do or say something that is peaceful. You may want to encourage the activity all year long, supplying new balls as necessary.

LISTEN! LISTEN! HEAR THAT SOUND?

Initial	Medial	Final
August	bought	claw
auk	cause	draw
Austin	football	guffaw
author	install	jaw
authority	overhaul	jigsaw
automobile	Paula	straw
ought	Saul	thaw
	shawl	
	taught	
	thought	

Rubber Band Ball

One little rubber band
was not enough at all
to loop on my eraser
for a rubber band ball.

I took one from our celery,
the paper in the hall,
and a band from 'round our doorknob
for a rubber band ball.

I twisted and I wrapped them.
They wound up very small.
Four rubber bands were not enough,
just not enough at all!

I hunted and I found some more
at school and in the mall.
My friends began to help me
make a rubber band ball.

Our ball grew rounder, rounder.
Now my friends all like to call,
"Hey, bounce a super high one—
It's a rubber band ball!"

Sydnie Meltzer Kleinhenz

Other Vowel Sounds:

a

a

A Walk in Fall

by
Lois Muehl

TARGETED SOUND

Vowel **a** as in **ball/ought/claw:** walk, fall, grandpa, call, walking, talk, walnuts, ball, stall, haul

(See also Diphthong *au/aw* as in *haul/claw.*)

ADDITIONAL SOUNDS

Consonant **l** as in **long:** fall, likes, call, whole, walnuts, below, pull, ball, squirrels', leave, look, stall, squirrels, haul

Long vowel **e** as in **me:** me, he, we, see, leave

Long vowel **i** as in **like:** my, sometimes, likes, time, ripen, I

Long vowel **o** as in **rope:** slows, so, whole, shows, grow, below

Short vowels: in, sometimes, and, his, can, on, walnuts, husk, but, back, begin

FOCUSING TALK

- Innovate on the poem's words as needed to tell about someone in your life with whom you go walking.

- Talk about how a walnut rests inside its shell, inside a husk. Then compare the husking and shelling of a walnut to your own or a child's removal of layers of clothing. Similar comparisons might be made to uncovering a seed inside of a fruit, finding a game inside of a file on a computer disk, or revealing each layer of a stack of nested containers.

ACTIVITY: AN AWESOME WALK

Take an autumn walk to look for seasonal signs, such as walnuts on the ground, acorns, dried leaves, squirrels, or pumpkins—all as signs of fall. Collect mementos from the walk and display them under a caption "An Awesome Walk." Add illustrations for sightings such as squirrels or trees that are "decked out" for the season. Repeat for a walk in spring, summer, or winter.

LISTEN! LISTEN! HEAR THAT SOUND?

Initial	Medial		Final
all	appalling	Guatemala	caw
auburn	brought	mall	flaw
audio	calling	small	raw
awesome	caught	sought	saw
awful	crawl		slaw
awfully	eyeball		

A Walk in Fall

My grandpa sometimes likes to call
and take me walking in the fall.

He slows his pace so we can talk.
We talk the whole time on our walk.

He shows me where the walnuts grow
And ripen 'fore they fall below.

We pull a husk and see a ball.
My grandpa says, "Squirrels' food in fall."

We leave, but I look back and stall
To watch the squirrels begin their haul.

Lois Muehl

Other Vowel Sounds:

a

Bulldog Bully

by
Babs Bell Hajdusiewicz

TARGETED SOUND

Vowel **u** as in **full:**

Bulldog, bully, neighborhood's, bullied, pullets, bulls, ambushed, bull-headed, pushed, bushes

ADDITIONAL SOUNDS

Consonant **b** as in **boy:**

Bulldog, bully, Billy, neighborhood's, bullied, baby, bulls, but, ambushed, bullheaded, bushes, Billy's

Consonant **d** as in **dad:**

Bulldog, neighborhood's, field, instead, head

Ending **-d/-ed** as in **hoped/waited:**

bullied, ambushed, bullheaded, pushed

FOCUSING TALK

- Tell children about a person or an animal you've known who acted like a bully. Describe the bully's actions, and how those actions affected the bully *and* others.

- Introduce children to a different and more positive use of the word *bully* with the saying "Bully for you!" as you praise their accomplishments.

ACTIVITY: LISTEN UP, BULLY!

Draw or cut out a picture of a bulldog or bullfrog. Display the picture and invite children to suggest helpful words one might say to help a bully understand how bullying behavior makes others feel. Write children's words as captions and post the captions all around the "bully" as helpful reminders.

LISTEN! LISTEN! HEAR THAT SOUND?

Medial
bullet
bullhorn
bulrush
Pulitzer
pull
Pullam
pullover
pulpit

Bulldog Bully

Bulldog Billy was the neighborhood's bully.
    He bullied everything in sight.
He bullied all the pullets till they ran to roost,
    Then he bullied baby frogs all night.

Billy tried to bully two bulls in a field,
    But Billy got ambushed, instead.
Two bullheaded bulls pushed Billy in the bushes—
    Now Billy's off nursing his head.

Babs Bell Hajdusiewicz

Other Vowel Sounds:

u

u

u

Shouldn't, Couldn't, Wouldn't

by
Carol Murray

u

u

u

u

TARGETED SOUND

Vowel **u** as in **full:**

shouldn't, couldn't wouldn't

(See also vowel digraph *oo* as in *book.*)

ADDITIONAL SOUNDS

Consonant **t** as in **top:**

shouldn't, couldn't, wouldn't, that, it, isn't, it's, not, doesn't, right, neat, feet

Contractions:

shouldn't, couldn't wouldn't, isn't, it's, doesn't

FOCUSING TALK

▪ Quote any of the poem's first five lines when you're weighing the pros and cons of an action.

▪ Innovate on the poem's last lines to model the importance of washing hands before eating. For example, you might say, "Soiled hands mustn't touch yummy food I will eat," or "Dirty hands shouldn't touch any food I will eat."

ACTIVITY: I SHOULDN'T . . .

Invite children to illustrate something they shouldn't do but are tempted to do. Help each child write a sentence that begins with "I Shouldn't" to tell about the picture.

LISTEN! LISTEN! HEAR THAT SOUND?

Medial
bull
bulldozer
bulletin
bullfighter
bullfrog
bullish
fulfill
pudding
pull
pulltoy
push
put
should
would

Shouldn't, Couldn't, Wouldn't

I know that I shouldn't—
  It just isn't done.
It's not that I *couldn't*—
  It wouldn't be fun.
It doesn't seem right.
  It's also not neat—
Clean socks shouldn't go
  on my smelly old feet.

Carol Murray

Other Vowel Sounds:

u

OO

It's Fishy

by
Babs Bell Hajdusiewicz

TARGETED SOUND

Vowel digraph **oo** as in **book:**

book, look, cook, hook

(See also *u* as in *full.*)

ADDITIONAL SOUND

Consonant **k**/hard **c** as in **kite/cat:**

book, look, cook, hook

FOCUSING TALK

▪ Innovate on the poem's text to talk about a book you used to locate some information: "This morning I *opened* this book. . . ."

▪ Borrow from the poem's words to say, "That would mean *me* on the hook!" when you feel you may be "pushed" into taking responsibility for another's actions. Use the words similarly to say, "That would mean *you* on the hook!" when a child's ownership of responsibility is in question.

ACTIVITY: A FISHY COOKBOOK

Invite children to bring in favorite recipes for fish dishes. Arrange the recipes, along with children's illustrations or cut-out pictures, to create a cookbook. Make copies for each child to share at home.

LISTEN! LISTEN! HEAR THAT SOUND?

Medial
cooker
cookout
could
foot
good
hood
poof
poor
wood
wool

It's Fishy

This morning I borrowed this book
To look for new dinners to cook.
      But every new dish
      Included a fish
And that would mean *me* on the hook!

Babs Bell Hajdusiewicz

Other Vowel Sounds:

oo
Mantis-Hood

by
Norma Farber

TARGETED SOUND

Vowel digraph **oo** as in **book:**

mantis-hood, book, look, good, should

(See also *u* as in *full.*)

ADDITIONAL SOUNDS

Blends:

mantis-hood, praying, mantis, children, grow, properly, and

Consonant digraph **sh** as in **ship:**

shoulder, should

FOCUSING TALK

▪ Quoting the poem's words, "It says in a book . . . ," can be a good way to respond to children's questions *and* simultaneously model how information comes from books. At times, you'll want to substitute *magazine* or *newspaper* for *book.*

▪ Utilize the poem's words as a gentle reminder to encourage positive behavior. Once children are familiar with the poem and its meaning, you may find you can simply say, "Said the praying mantis . . ." and children will finish the line for you *and* begin to exhibit positive behaviors.

ACTIVITY: THE "GOOD" BOOK

Invite children to draw or cut out pictures to illustrate their ideas of "being good." Compile the pictures to make a book titled *The "Good" Book.*

LISTEN! LISTEN! HEAR THAT SOUND?

Medial
cookie
hoof
rookie
shook
songbook
stood
took
wooded
woof
would

Mantis-Hood

Said the praying mantis: It says in a book,
over my shoulder I'm able to look.
Over my shoulder (it's said by a man),
look back, I'm the *only* insect that can.

Said the praying mantis: My Children, be good.
Grow up to do all that you properly should.
Grow into your mantis-hood wiser and older,
so you will be fit to look over your shoulder.

Norma Farber

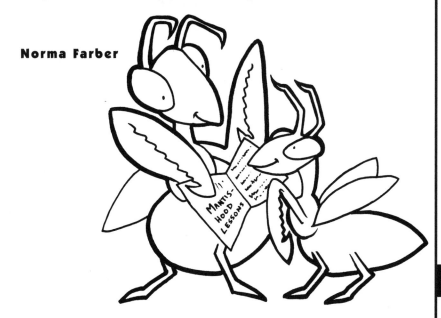

a

a

Lizard
Longing

by
Tony Johnston

a

a

a

a

a

TARGETED SOUND

Schwa **a** as in **mama:**

> gonna, Mama, iguana, piranha, flora, fauna

ADDITIONAL SOUNDS

Contractions:

> I'm, don't, I'd

FOCUSING TALK

▪ Play on the poem's language to talk about other wants. For example, you might say, "I'm gonna tell Mother I want a new brother," or "I'm gonna tell Santa I want some new pants-a."

▪ Use the word *flora* to talk about a group of plants. Similarly, talk about the *fauna,* or group of animals in a story or at the zoo. At another time, use the poem's rhythm and ideas to model opposites for children by talking about what you *don't* want and what you'd *rather* have.

ACTIVITY: FLORA AND FAUNA

Provide dried flowers and miniature animal toys, or use pictures of flowers and animals, and have children sort them by size, habitat, color, or another characteristic, into several groups of flora and fauna.

LISTEN! LISTEN! HEAR THAT SOUND?

Initial	Medial	Final
account	doable	Cuba
accuse	hippopotamus	hula
acquaint	lackadaisical	pasta
again	loveable	puma
against	macaroon	tuna
aghast	magazine	Yuma
ago	manager	
ahead	signature	
alike		
away		

Lizard Longing

I'm gonna tell Mama
I want an iguana,
all blinky and scaly
just like a piranha.
I don't want some flora,
I'd rather have fauna.
I'm gonna tell Mama
I want an iguana.

Tony Johnston

Seven Children

by
Sydnie Meltzer Kleinhenz

TARGETED SOUNDS

Schwa **a** as in **mama:**

around, away, amount, disappointment, idea

Schwa **e** as in **taken:**

seven, children, uneven

Schwa **o** as in **lemon:**

mayonnaise

ADDITIONAL SOUND

Diphthong **ou** as in **out/cow:**

around, found, ground, amount, count,

FOCUSING TALK

▪ Quote the poem's line, "A good idea made things fair," when children's ideas work to solve disputes. Similarly, the poem's lines, "With plans to split the full amount," and "Uneven shares for every friend caused disappointment," might be quoted when children are sharing or *not* sharing.

▪ Substitute other numbers and adjectives to innovate on the poem's last line, "And cut it seven scrumptious ways," when you or children are dividing any number of things.

ACTIVITY: SHARED AMOUNTS

Provide seven containers along with a number of coins, seeds, beans, or cereal pieces. Have children experiment with dividing the items equally among the containers. Which numbers allow for seven uneven shares? Which allow for seven even shares?

LISTEN! LISTEN! HEAR THAT SOUND?

Initial	Medial		Final
observe	elephant	imitate	encyclopedia
offend	engineer	material	Formica
opinion	favorite	octopus	Oklahoma
oppose	feminine	often	orchestra
original	festival	Oklahoma	Ottawa
	flammable	practical	
	formal	residence	

Seven Children

Seven children played around
Till one found money on the ground.
Then seven children quit their play
And seven children searched away.

With plans to split the full amount,
The seven children took a count.
Uneven shares for every friend
Caused disappointment.
In the end,

A good idea made things fair.
The seven children, glad to share,
Bought ham on rye with mayonnaise
And cut it seven scrumptious ways.

Sydnie Meltzer Kleinhenz

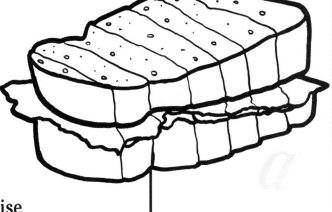

Other Vowel Sounds:

a

y

y

Four Seasons

by
Anonymous

y

y *y*

y

y

y

TARGETED SOUND

Consonant **y** as **e** as in **very:**

> showery, flowery, bowery, hoppy, choppy, poppy, wheezy, sneezy, freezy, slippy, drippy, nippy

ADDITIONAL SOUNDS

Blends:

> spring, flowery, sneezy, freezy, slippy, drippy

R-controlled vowel **ur** as in **hurt:**

> showery, flowery, bowery, summer, winter

FOCUSING TALK

▪ Add to the poem real or coined words that include the targeted sound and use them to describe each season. For example, spring might also be described as "springy" or "blustery," while summer might be "sunny," "funny," or "scorchy." Likewise, think about autumn as being "pumpkin-y," "leafy," or "squirrel-y," and winter as being "blustery," slippery," or "holiday-y."

▪ Innovate on the text to describe other ideas, such as the months of the year, individual children, or places children like to visit. Ask children to think about whether the descriptions fit as you substitute other words or names for each these. For example, Darleen might be "showery, flowery, bowery," while the zoo might be "wheezy, sneezy, freezy," if visited on a cool day. At another time, talk about the word *seasonings* and have children help choose four seasonings or spices that they then describe with words that include the targeted sound.

ACTIVITY: FOUR SEASONS

Invite children's help in preparing a bulletin board display about the seasons. Use the poem's words as captions for illustrations children draw or cut out from magazines.

LISTEN! LISTEN! HEAR THAT SOUND?

Medial	Final	
anything	baby	many
babysitter	copy	only
bodyguard	funny	pretty
everyone	healthy	very
ladybug	January	

Four Seasons

Spring is showery, flowery, bowery.
Summer: hoppy, choppy, poppy.
Autumn: wheezy, sneezy, freezy.
Winter: slippy, drippy, nippy.

Anonymous

Other Vowel Sounds:

y

y

Hunky-dunky Donkey

by
J. Patrick Lewis

TARGETED SOUND

Consonant **y** as **e** as in **very:**

hunk-dunky, donkey, monkey, Spanky, Dinky, funky, hunky-dory, story

ADDITIONAL SOUNDS

Final blend **-nk** as in **pink:**

hunky-dunky, donkey, monkey, Spanky, Dinky, funky, hunky-dory

Short vowels:

hunky-dunky, was, monkey, Spanky, met, donkey, Dinky, had, funky, hunky-dory, of, asked, if, his

 ### FOCUSING TALK

▪ Begin an interesting personal story this way: "I have a funky, hunky-dory story to tell."

▪ Innovate on the text to explore other names that end in the sound of *y* as *e*. For example, the monkey or donkey might be named Huey, Lindy, Hillary, Nicky, Brandy, or Jamey.

 ### ACTIVITY: A HUNKY-DUNKY STORY

Invite children to illustrate the poem as a book. The first page might include the poem's first five words with a picture of a monkey. Pages 2 and 3 might include the next five words with a picture of a donkey. Several pages might then show the animals' "funky hunky-dory story sort of life," etc.

 ### LISTEN! LISTEN! HEAR THAT SOUND?

Medial	Final	
any time	berry	Mary
anywhere	bunny	monopoly
baby sit	city	party
funny bone	enemy	pony
	energy	Tony
	honey	

Hunky-dunky Donkey

There
was a
monkey,
Spanky,
who met
a donkey,
Dinky.
They
had a
funky
hunky-
dory
story
sort of
life,
Because
the
monkey,
Spanky,
had asked
the donkey,
Dinky,
if she
would
be his
hunky-
dunky
donkey
sort of
wife.

J. Patrick Lewis

Other Vowel Sounds:

y

y

My Puppy

by
Aileen Fisher

TARGETED SOUND

Consonant **y** as **e** as in **very:**

puppy, funny, happy, yappy, grumpy, slumpy

ADDITIONAL SOUNDS

Short vowel **a** as in **cat:**

happy, yappy, and, an, at

Short vowel **u** as in **rug:**

puppy, funny, just, grumpy, slumpy, such

FOCUSING TALK

▪ Quote the poem to tell about your or a friend's dog. At other times, change *my* to *your* to talk about a child's dog, or change *puppy* to *kitten, hamster,* or any other pet. Comment on how some of the poem's ideas don't make sense when talking about other kinds of pets.

▪ Say, "I'm happy and yappy!" when you're feeling a burst of happiness. When appropriate, comment on how you or a child seems to be feeling "grumpy and slumpy."

ACTIVITY: MY PUPPY

Ask children to think about a puppy they know or one they would like to know. Provide clay for children to use in making likenesses of their puppy friends. Help children recite the poem or innovate on its words to tell about their clay puppies.

LISTEN! LISTEN! HEAR THAT SOUND?

Medial	Final
anyone	empty
anything	entry
busybody	funny
honeybun	harmony
	Henry
	honesty
	Jenny
	money
	naughty
	penny
	Sherry

My Puppy

It's funny
my puppy
knows just how I feel.

When I'm happy
he's yappy
and squirms like an eel.

When I'm grumpy
he's slumpy
and stays at my heel.

It's funny
my puppy
knows such a great deal.

Aileen Fisher

y
Why?

by
Ellen Javernick

TARGETED SOUND
Consonant **y** as **i** as in **sky:**

sky, why, fly, imply, shy, spy, my, nearby

ADDITIONAL SOUNDS
Blends:

sky, fly, imply, spy

Consonant digraphs:

why, this, the, that, shy

FOCUSING TALK
▪ When appropriate, confirm your interpretation of a child's statement or question by asking, "Does this imply that. . . ?"

▪ Children will enjoy your playing with the poem's words when you respond to their raised hands by asking, "Does this imply that you need help, or should I wait until you yelp?"

ACTIVITY: THIS IMPLIES . . .
Have children cut out pictures of people involved in various activities. Help children "read between the lines" to tell what the people might have done before the picture was taken, how the person was feeling during the photo shoot, or what might have happened afterward. Ask children to use picture clues along with their own experiences to explain their ideas.

LISTEN! LISTEN! HEAR THAT SOUND?
Final
apply
butterfly
classify
eye
fry
guy
lullaby
qualify
verify

Why?

Oh, little bird up in the sky,
Why do you fly so high,
       so high?
Does this imply that you are shy?
Or did you spy my cat nearby?

Ellen Javernick

y

y

Cry, Sky!

by
Babs Bell Hajdusiewicz

TARGETED SOUND

Consonant **y** as **i** as in **sky:**

cry, sky, try, why, dry

ADDITIONAL SOUNDS

Blends:

cry, sky, please, try, dry

 ### FOCUSING TALK

▪ Recite the poem while looking at a classroom plant that needs watering. Of course, you can expect children to tell you that that doesn't make sense for an indoor plant!

▪ Preserving the poem's rhythm and its persuasive tone, innovate on the text as follows to encourage a child to try harder at a task: "(child's name), please try. Please try to (name activity). I'll tell you why. . . ."

 ### ACTIVITY: DRYING OUT

Provide a sponge, a sheet of paper toweling, a washcloth, and a dish towel or hand towel. Have children lay the items flat and side-by-side. Pour the same amount of water on each item and then check the items periodically to see how much time elapses until each dries out.

 ### LISTEN! LISTEN! HEAR THAT SOUND?

Final
amplify
bye
imply
multiply
nearby
rely
satisfy
sly

Cry, Sky!

Sky, please cry.
Please try to cry.
I'll tell you why—
The Earth is dry.

Babs Bell Hajdusiewicz

Plurals

-s as in ***dogs***

-es as in ***boxes***

-ies as in ***babies***

Possessives

's as in ***dad's***

s/es/ies

es

Twenty-four Things That I Like Best

(And two that I don't)

by
Katherine Burton

TARGETED SOUND

Plural **-s/-es/-ies** as in **dogs/boxes/babies:** things, seashells, puppies, kittens, rocks, apples, hot dogs, shoes, socks, mudpies, marbles, cupcakes, cars, sand castles, jawbreakers, stars, jellybeans, rockets, bananas, spots, rainbows, turtles, astronauts, bicycles, snowflakes, feathers, fleas, kites, trees, pools, degrees

ADDITIONAL SOUNDS

Long vowels: I, like, seashells, shoes, mudpies, cupcakes, jawbreakers, jellybeans, rainbows, brave, bicycles, snowflakes, fleas, kites, they, fly, trees, degrees

Short vowels: twenty-four, things, that, best, and, seashells, puppies, kittens, rocks, apples, hot dogs, without, socks, mudpies, cupcakes, sand castles, wishing, on, jellybeans, rockets, bananas, with, spots, astronauts, bicycles, feathers, when, stuck, in, swimming, it's, one-hundred

FOCUSING TALK

▪ Describe a positive behavior as one of the twenty-four things you like best and children will want to help name the other twenty-three! Or, refer to a negative behavior as one of the two things you *don't* like.

▪ Help children identify the two things the poet doesn't like (banana with spots, fleas). Talk about how the poet "hid" her dislikes in the poem, much like we prefer to "hide" or not have to "face" things we dislike. Then try to name twenty-four things that you don't like and talk about how it's sometimes easier to name things you like than to name dislikes.

ACTIVITY: "24 THINGS THAT I LIKE BEST" BOOK

Invite children to cut out or draw pictures of favorite things and to collectively make a book. Children might place one picture on each page and "hide" among the "likes" two pictures of things they don't like.

LISTEN! LISTEN! HEAR THAT SOUND?

Final -s	-es	-ies
books	benches	berries
dinosaurs	buses	bunnies
houses	dishes	countries
radios	inches	cries
walls	peaches	puppies
windows	quizzes	stories

Twenty-four Things
That I Like Best
(And two that I don't)

Seashells and puppies,
kittens and rocks,
apples and hot dogs,
shoes without socks.

Mudpies and marbles,
cupcakes and cars,
sand castles, jawbreakers,
wishing on stars.

Jellybeans, rockets,
bananas with spots,
rainbows and turtles,
and brave astronauts.

Bicycles, snowflakes,
feathers and fleas,
kites . . . when they fly
'stead of stuck in the trees.

And swimming pools when it's one-hundred degrees.

Katherine Burton

Plurals:

s/es/ies

es

Ears Hear

by
Lucia and James
L. Hymes, Jr.

s
es
ies
es
ies
s

TARGETED SOUND

Plural **-s/-es/-ies** as in **dogs/boxes/babies:**

> ears, flies, motors, kettles, dogs, birds, autos, winds, shoes, trucks, floors, whistles, bells, doors, kids, clocks, babies, phones, balls, spoons

ADDITIONAL SOUNDS

Final blend **-ng** as in **sing:**

> clang, bang, ding, ring

S-blends:

> snore, squeak, slam, spoons, scream

FOCUSING TALK

▪ Comment on sounds you hear by engaging children this way: "My ears hear. . . ." You might use this introductory statement to note children's laughter, the sounds of helpful tidying up, or cooperative talk aimed at preventing or resolving a conflict. Similarly, you'll find this approach helpful in ending disruptive sounds.

▪ Follow the poem's format and rhythm to comment on objects around you. For example, you might say, "Doors close, windows lock, eyes watch a ticking clock," or "Pencils write, papers blow, bells ring, kids go."

ACTIVITY: EARS HEAR

Cut two large sheets of paper into the shape of ears. Attach one ear shape high on a wall on one side of the room and the other ear shape high on an opposite wall. Attach a string from one ear to the other. Have children draw or cut out pictures to illustrate sounds in the room that the ears might hear. Use clothespins or paper clips to attach the pictures along the string.

LISTEN! LISTEN! HEAR THAT SOUND?

Final

-s	-es	-ies
brooms	brushes	flies
crows	buzzes	ponies
days	foxes	poppies
months	lunches	skies
weeks	ranches	tummies
wiggles	zeroes	worries

Ears Hear

Flies buzz,
Motors roar.
Kettles hiss,
People snore.
Dogs bark,
Birds cheep.
Autos honk: *Beep! Beep!*

Winds sigh,
Shoes squeak.
Trucks honk,
Floors creak.
Whistles toot,
Bells clang.
Doors slam: *Bang! Bang!*

Kids shout,
Clocks ding.
Babies cry,
Phones ring.
Balls bounce,
Spoons drop.
People scream: *Stop! Stop!*

Lucia and James L. Hymes, Jr.

Plurals:

s/es/ies

es

**But
I Wonder . . .**

by
Aileen Fisher

s

es

ies

es

ies

s

TARGETED SOUND

Plural **-s/-es/-ies** as in **dogs/boxes/babies:**

crickets, thickets, katydids, trees, ants, plants, butterflies, ladybugs, bees, noses, feelers

ADDITIONAL SOUNDS

Long vowels:

I, katydids, trees, butterflies, ladybugs, bees, don't, noses, feelers, you, please, they, quite, nicely, sneeze

Short vowel **i** as in **pin:**

crickets, in, thickets, katydids, with, little, if

FOCUSING TALK

▪ Quote the poem's last two lines, "They get along quite nicely, but I wonder how they *sneeze*," when children are working or playing together, or when you spy a group of ants or other insects.

▪ Children will enjoy your innovation on the poem when a food aroma is detected. For example, you might say, "We smell with little noses, *not* with feelers, if you please!"

ACTIVITY: BUTTERFLIES

Have children fold a sheet of paper in half. Lay the paper with the fold on the left. Begin at the top of the folded edge and draw a large numeral 3 on the paper, ending at the bottom of the folded edge. Cut on the drawn lines and unfold the paper to see a butterfly. Let children decorate as desired. Show children how to press and release a paper butterfly at the fold to make the wings "flap."

LISTEN! LISTEN! HEAR THAT SOUND?

Final

-s	**-es**	**-ies**
monkeys	bosses	cherries
peanuts	coaches	dairies
pets	gashes	dragonflies
schools	jellyfishes	pennies
shoppers	matches	
troubles	passes	
	sixes	

But I Wonder . . .

The crickets in the thickets,
and the katydids in trees,
and ants on plants, and butterflies,
and ladybugs and bees
don't smell with little noses
but with *feelers,* if you please.
They get along quite nicely,
but I wonder how they *sneeze.*

Aileen Fisher

Plurals:

s/es/ies

'S

'S

Mama's Present

by
Babs Bell Hajdusiewicz

'S 'S

'S

'S

'S

TARGETED SOUND

Possessive **'s** as in **dad's:**

> Grandma's, Sister's, Grandpa's, neighbor's, people's, Mama's

ADDITIONAL SOUNDS

Contraction:

> I'm

Ending **-ing** as in **going:**

> using, wearing, hoping

FOCUSING TALK

▪ Introduce children to the saying "Money doesn't grow on trees." Talk about how this is often said to someone who spends money too freely.

▪ Talk about a time when you gave a gift, such as candy, and hoped the person might share with you. Discuss how people often give gifts they would actually like to keep for themselves. Help children recognize that this makes sense, since choosing a gift for someone often means we like it ourselves.

ACTIVITY: MONEY TREE

Provide pennies, cans or margarine tubs, foil wrap, and small twigs with branches. Children can plant the twigs in foil-wrapped cans or tubs and then tape or glue pennies onto the twigs. Encourage children to give their gifts to loved ones.

LISTEN! LISTEN! HEAR THAT SOUND?

Final
body's
bus's
children's
class's
computer's
dog's
finger's
person's
principal's
teacher's

Mama's Present

I'm using Grandma's pennies,
And I'm wearing Sister's shirt.
And I'm using Grandpa's shovel
And the neighbor's twig and dirt.

I'm using other people's things
To make this money tree.
I'm hoping Mama's gift will grow—
And she will share with me.

Babs Bell Hajdusiewicz

Possessives:

's

's

's

Whose Shoes?

by
Lucinda Cave

TARGETED SOUND

Possessive **'s** as in **dad's:**

Surd's, Abby's, Carmen's, Gabby's, Miko's, Kevin's, Carrie's, Jerry's, Barry's, Devon's, nobody's

ADDITIONAL SOUNDS

R-controlled vowels:

wore, Carmen's, Carmen, Carrie's, Jerry's, Barry's, barefooted

Short vowels:

if, Andrew, and, Abby's, Abby, Carmen's, Carmen, Gabby's, Gabby, Kevin's, Devon's, then, on, nobody's, friend's, running, next

FOCUSING TALK

▪ Quote the line, "whose shoes would these be—on *nobody's* feet?" when you see a pair of shoes out of place.

▪ Substitute children's names in the poem and innovate on the words to fit the situation. For example, you might reference the poem when children are shoeless in the gym or in the hall.

ACTIVITY: WHOSE SHOES?

Have children cut out pictures of shoe pairs from old magazines and catalogs. Help children cut the pairs in half and then match up pairs. Ask children whether a male or female might wear each pair. Ask children what age person might wear each pair of shoes.

LISTEN! LISTEN! HEAR THAT SOUND?

Final
coat's
grandpa's
lamp's
mind's
mom's
neighbor's
parent's
picture's
recipe's
shoe's

Whose Shoes?

If Andrew wore Sudra's
and Sudra wore Abby's
and Abby wore Carmen's
and Carmen wore Gabby's;
If Gabby wore Miko's
and Miko wore Kevin's
or Carrie's
or Jerry's
or Barry's
or Devon's—
Then whose shoes would these be—
on *nobody's* feet?

What friend's running barefooted
next to the street?

Lucinda Cave

Possessives:

's

R-controlled Vowels

ar as in **park**
or as in **sort**
ur as in **hurt**

R-controlled Vowel Digraphs

air as in **pair**
ear/eer/ier as in **hear/deer/pier**
our/owr as in **hour/power**

ar

What Dog Would?

by
Sydnie Meltzer Kleinhenz

TARGETED SOUND

R-controlled vowel **ar** as in **park:**

> guard, start, yard, dark, hardy, bark, large, harmless

ADDITIONAL SOUND

Consonant **d** as in **dad:**

> dog, would, guard, yard, outside, dark, hardy, dogwood

FOCUSING TALK

▪ Use the poem's rhythm to create riddles about other uses of the word *dog*. Examples might include these: What dog would never bark or climb, but feeds me well at dinnertime? (hot dog); What dog's the messiest to hold, and sounds like it is very cold? (chili dog); What dog might show me where to look, but does great damage to a book? (dog-ear); What dog would never hurt a flea, but helps me swim quite easily? (dog paddle); What dog will carry home the meat when stomachs feel too full to eat? (doggie bag).

▪ Talk about a dog you've known that had a "hardy bark," or a dog that would *quickly* start to leave the yard. You might also innovate on the poem to say, "It's tame and harmless as a tree," to encourage children to try something new.

ACTIVITY: WHAT DOG WOULD?

Provide three large sheets of paper or poster board. Draw or cut out three pictured settings as follows: a doghouse or a dog's bed, for a dog; a hot dog bun or hot dog vendor's cart, for a hot dog; a forest or yard, for a tree. Then have children draw or cut out several pictures of dogs, hot dogs, and dogwood trees. Invite children to place each pictured "dog" in its appropriate setting.

LISTEN! LISTEN! HEAR THAT SOUND?

Initial	Medial	Final
Arctic	barnyard	bar
are	card	car
arm	charred	far
army	farm	jar
art	garden	star
artist	hard	tar
	March	
	part	
	party	

What Dog Would?

What dog would stand as if to guard
And never start to leave our yard?

    Our dog would.

What dog would stay outside at dark
And always have a hardy bark?

    Our dog would.

What dog would grow quite large, but be
As tame and harmless as a tree?

    Our *dogwood!*

Sydnie Meltzer Kleinhenz

R-Controlled Vowels:

ar

ar

Hardy Har Har!

by
Babs Bell Hajdusiewicz

TARGETED SOUND

R-controlled vowel **ar** as in **park:**

Hardy har har, Aardwolf, Arnie, aardvark, guard, park, hard, argued, dark

ADDITIONAL SOUNDS

Other **r**-controlled vowels:

for, nocturnal, hire

FOCUSING TALK

▪ Children will enjoy your humor as you yawn and say, "I think I'll sleep through the day and wake when it's dark!" At another time, you might motivate a tired child by saying, "Let's *work* through the day and *sleep* when it's dark!" Also, children will enjoy sharing stories about baby siblings who might be called "nocturnal" since they're often up all night.

▪ Innovate on the poem's words to comment on who's been "hired" for each classroom duty for the week and why. For instance, you might say, "(child's name) is a good organizer. That's why we've hired him/her to keep the bookshelves organized this week."

ACTIVITY: NIGHT GUARDS

Provide newspapers, catalogs, and old nature magazines. Children will enjoy drawing or cutting out pictures of people dressed as guards, along with pictures of bats, aardvarks, and hyenas, to create a display of "Night Guards" who watch over the room when children are at home sleeping. Don't forget to include some pictures of "up-all-night" babies (and their parents or siblings) in the display!

LISTEN! LISTEN! HEAR THAT SOUND?

Initial	Medial	Final
arbor	courtyard	bazaar
arch	discard	czar
argument	hardy	guitar
ark	large	jaguar
artery	postcard	scar
article	start	streetcar
	tardy	
	yard	

Hardy Har Har!

Both Aardwolf Hyena
And Arnie Aardvark
Applied for guard jobs
At night in the park.

"But, Aardwolf Hyena,
A night job is hard!
You must be nocturnal
To be a night guard!
They'll only hire me,"
Argued Arnie Aardvark.
"I sleep through the day
And wake when it's dark."

"Well, Hardy Har Har!
I sleep all day, too!"
Laughed Aardwolf Hyena.
"I'm nocturnal, like you!"

Babs Bell Hajdusiewicz

R-Controlled Vowels:

ar

or

or

Pig Out on Pork

by
Sydnie Meltzer Kleinhenz

or

or

or

or

TARGETED SOUND

R-controlled vowel **or** as in **sort:**

pork, gorge, sorts, gorging, your, roar, remorse, hoarse

ADDITIONAL SOUND

Consonant **g** as in **go:**

pig, gorge, big, gorging, piggies

FOCUSING TALK

▪ You'll want to be sure children recognize the humor suggested by the homophone *hoarse/horse* in the poem's line ". . . and then become a little hoarse." Children will enjoy your use of the word *gorge* when you or someone is enjoying a favorite food. You might also use the word when someone is using too much glue or other material. Similarly, use the word *remorse* when you or a child is feeling regretful.

▪ Innovate on the poem's first five lines to encourage children to utilize learning tools, such as writing paper or books. For example, you might display writing paper in many sizes and say, "Gorge on paper, small to big. All sorts of choices. Be a pig."

ACTIVITY: A PORKY PICTURE

Draw or copy a large picture of a pig. Help children cut out pictures of food products that come from pigs and place each picture in its appropriate place on the pig. For example, bacon comes from the jowl or belly of the pig, pork loin and pork chops from the pig's back, ribs from the rib area, pork steak from the upper legs, lard from the upper head area, pigs' feet from the feet, and ham from the pig's rear end.

LISTEN! LISTEN! HEAR THAT SOUND?

Initial	Medial	Final
or	born	before
orbit	forget	bore
orchestra	fork	for
order	glorious	four
ordinary	horn	more
ore	short	nor
		score

Pig Out on Pork

Gorge on
pig meat,
small to big.
All sorts of choices.
Be a pig.
And while
you're gorging,
do not eat
those little piggies
on your feet,
for you would roar
with true remorse
and then become
a little hoarse.

Sydnie Meltzer Kleinhenz

R-Controlled Vowels:

or

or

or

The dinosaur dinner

by
Dennis Lee

or

or or

or

or

or

TARGETED SOUND

R-controlled vowel **or** as in **sort:**

dinosaur, allosaurus, stegosaurus, brontosaurus, for, Tyrannosaurus

ADDITIONAL SOUNDS

Consonant **s** as in **so/city:**

dinosaur, allosaurus, stegosaurus, brontosaurus, tyrannosaurus

Schwa **o** as in **lemon:**

dinosaur, allosaurus, stegosaurus, brontosaurus, tyrannosaurus

FOCUSING TALK

▪ Children asking for your help will enjoy hearing you say, "Along comes the teacher called (your name)." Similarly, you might announce children's departure for lunch by saying, "All went off for munching at the cafeteria room."

▪ As children form groups for various activities, invite them to use a dinosaur's name for each group. Then quote or innovate on the poem to comment on children's going off to do an activity.

ACTIVITY: DINOSAUR SORT

Cut out or copy pictures of dinosaurs from old magazines or catalogs, or invite children to bring in toy dinosaurs. Have children sort the pictures or toy dinosaurs by type. Children will also enjoy using the pictures or toys to reenact the poem's story.

LISTEN! LISTEN! HEAR THAT SOUND?

Initial	Medial	Final
oral	form	adore
orb	George	drawer
orchid	important	floor
ordeal	porch	roar
Oregon	porridge	short
Oreo®	stork	store
organ	storm	wore
	story	your

The dinosaur dinner

Allosaurus, stegosaurus,
Brontosaurus too,
All went off for dinner at the
Dinosaur zoo.

Along came the waiter called
Tyrannosaurus Rex,
Gobbled up the table
'Cause they wouldn't pay their checks.

Dennis Lee

R-Controlled Vowels:

or

ur

ur

Thirty Dirty Turtles

by
Katherine Burton

TARGETED SOUND

R-controlled vowel **ur** as in **hurt:**

thirty, dirty, turtles, squirming, worming, turtle, squirt, turning, water, murky, jerking, churning, longer, gurgle

ADDITIONAL SOUND

Consonant **t** as in **top:**

thirty, dirty, turtles, tub, out, turtle, squirt, turning, water

FOCUSING TALK

▪ Innovate on the poem's words as appropriate when children are washing their hands. For example, when two children are cleaning up, you might say, "Twenty dirty fingers scrubbing in the sink . . . ," "Dirty, dirty fingers washing up for lunch . . . ," or "Very dirty water churning down the drain. . . ."

▪ Quote the poem's words, "Glug! Gurgle! Glug!" any time someone's getting a drink, when rainwater's gushing, or when water's going down a drain.

ACTIVITY: THIRTY (MORE OR LESS) TURTLES

Provide walnut-shell halves, paper scraps, and glue. Help children create turtles, using cut paper for heads and legs.

LISTEN! LISTEN! HEAR THAT SOUND?

Initial	Medial	Final
Earleen	burn	blur
ermine	curl	dinner
irk	derby	fur
Uruguay	nurse	murmur
urge	purple	occur
urgent	purse	were
	suburb	whir
	superb	wonder
	surface	
	Thursday	
	turn	

Thirty Dirty Turtles

Thirty dirty turtles
squirming
in a tub.

Worming out of
turtle shells—
Squirt!
Lather!
Scrub!

Turning water
murky.
Jerking
on the plug . . .

Ooops!

Thirty turtles
down
the
drain—
turning
churning
down
the
drain.
(No longer dirty)
Down
the
drain.

Gurgle!
Gurgle!
Glug!

Katherine Burton

R-Controlled Vowels:

ur

ur

ur
Bird Alert

by
Babs Bell Hajdusiewicz

ur ur ur ur

TARGETED SOUND

R-controlled vowel **ur** as in **hurt:** bird, alert, squirmy, worms, squirm, hurt, served, birds, dinner, dessert, turns, serving, dirt, blurt

ADDITIONAL SOUNDS

3-letter blend **squ** as in **squash:** squirmy, squirm

Consonant **d** as in **dad:** bird, birds, dinner, dessert, duty, dirt

Consonant **t** as in **top:** alert, at, thought, getting, hurt, to, dessert, take, turns, duty, dirt, blurt, out

FOCUSING TALK

▪ Innovate on the poem's words to issue a reminder, make an announcement, or register a request. For example, you might try "Lunch alert!" or "Cleanup alert!" to let children know it's time to get ready to go to lunch or go home, or "Homework alert!" to remind children of an assignment or a deadline.

▪ Quote the poem's words or innovate on them as appropriate to comment on children's activities, as when children are taking turns or when someone seems to be "squirming" as if trying to avoid an activity.

ACTIVITY: SQUIRMY-WORM ART

Provide containers of tempera paint in three or more different colors. Help children cut foot-long lengths of string, one for each paint container. Dip each string into its container, leaving one end clean for holding. Lift a paint-covered string and drop it onto a sheet of paper. Lift the string and drop it again. Repeat for other colors and let dry.

LISTEN! LISTEN! HEAR THAT SOUND?

Initial	Medial	Final
Earl	birthday	burr
early	circus	fir
urban	dirty	her
urchin	first	prefer
urn	girl	sir
	heard	spur
	hurry	stir
	third	wander
	Virginia	
	word	

Bird Alert

Squirmy worms squirm
    at the thought of getting hurt,
Or being served to baby birds
    for dinner or dessert.

So squirmy worms take turns
    serving duty in the dirt.
A squirmy worm on bird patrol
    must blurt out, "Bird Alert!"

Babs Bell Hajdusiewicz

R-Controlled Vowels:

ur

Airfare

by
Babs Bell Hajdusiewicz

TARGETED SOUND

R-controlled vowel digraph **air** as in **pair:**

airfare, Sharon, Darin, fair, sparrows, there, air, care, fare

ADDITIONAL SOUNDS

Short vowels:

think, it's, that, can, travel, up, in, of, it, is, if, but, not, when, must

 FOCUSING TALK

■ Once children are familiar with the poem, use some of its lines to respond to children as appropriate. For example, when a child is being silly, you might say, "Oh, (child's name), you're joking!" When a child is heard saying "It's not fair!" you might inject a little humor (and distract the child) by saying, "Of course, it is fair. If *you* were a bird. . . ."

■ Invite children to participate in an imaginary trip that involves taking along some items whose names include the *air* sound. You might introduce the "trip" by saying, "In *January,* it will be *necessary* to travel by *air* to *Fairbanks.* It is *customary* for me to *carry* along a *very.* . . ." Items to take with you might include *raspberries,* a *scary bear, chairs,* a *nightmare* book, some fresh *air, underwear, a pear, repair* tools, a *pair* of socks, a *hairy* lion, *cherries,* a *fairly* large *carriage,* a *stereo,* and, of course, *parents* to pay the *airfare!*

 ACTIVITY: AIRFARES

Help children create sample airline tickets for trips they would like to take. Children might include on the ticket a picture of the destination, a seat number, the date issued, the dates of travel, and the ticket's cost.

 LISTEN! LISTEN! HEAR THAT SOUND?

Initial	Medial	Final
Aaron	carry	aware
air	January	bear
arid	merry	chair
Erin	necessary	millionaire
errand	raspberry	nightmare
	scary	prepare
	very	underwear
	voluntary	

Airfare

"Sharon," said Darin,
"I don't think it's fair
That sparrows can travel
Up there in the air."

"Oh, Darin, you're joking!
Of course, it is fair.
If *you* were a bird,
You'd fly in the air!"

"But, Sharon," said Darin,
"It's really *not* fair!
When *I* care to fly,
I must pay a fare!"

Babs Bell Hajdusiewicz

R-Controlled Digraphs:

air

air

air

What Clarissa Likes

by
Betsy Franco

air

air

air

air

air

TARGETED SOUND

R-controlled vowel digraph **air** as in **pair:** Clarissa, fair, hair, pair, stereos, wear, parents, airplane, everywhere, Clarissa's, affair, chair, care

ADDITIONAL SOUNDS

Blends: Clarissa, and, stereos, pretty, things, parents, airplane, travel, Clarissa's, most

Consonant digraphs: what, with, shaggy, she, things, they, everywhere, when, birthday, the, chair

Long vowels: likes, pony, she, stereos, to, own, airplane, they, everywhere, birthday, quite, huge, most, reading, read, knows, really

Short vowels: Clarissa, has, with, and, shaggy, of, pretty, things, an, travel, everywhere, when, comes, it's, but, is, in

FOCUSING TALK

▪ Draw on the poem to say, "What (child's name) likes most is . . . ," to comment on a child's obvious enjoyment of an activity. Similarly, when making a request or giving a child a compliment, you might substitute your name in the line to say, "What (your name) likes most is. . . ."

▪ Use words with the *air* sound to talk about your having made an error. You might say, for example, "I *care* that I made an *error,* so I need to *repair* my *error*."

ACTIVITY: WHAT I LIKE

Invite children to draw or cut out pictures to illustrate several things they like. Help children arrange their pictures to make individual books titled "What I Like." You might help children arrange their likes in order, with the favorite at the end of the book. Help children write "I like" above each picture, with the exception of the last, which might be annotated with the words, "But what (child's name) likes the most is. . . ."

LISTEN! LISTEN! HEAR THAT SOUND?

Initial	Medial	Final	
airfare	bury	care	stair
Arab	carriage	fare	their
area	cherry	mare	wear
Erica	February	pear	where
error	hairy	repair	
	Jerry		

What Clarissa Likes

Clarissa has a pony,
    with fair and shaggy hair.
She has a pair of stereos
    and pretty things to wear.

Her parents own an airplane.
    They travel everywhere.
And when Clarissa's birthday comes,
    it's quite a huge affair.

But what Clarissa likes the most
    is reading in a chair.
For when her parents read to her,
    she knows they *really* care.

Betsy Franco

air *air* *air* *air*

R-Controlled Digraphs:

air

ear

Circus Cheer

by
Jeanne B. Hargett

eer

ier

ear

eer

ier

TARGETED SOUND

R-controlled vowel digraph **ear/eer/ier** as in **hear/cheer/pier:**

> cheer, hear, rear, near, fearless, appear, volunteer, ears, cheers, souvenirs

ADDITIONAL SOUNDS

Blends:

> bands, stands, acrobat, swings, wings, clowns, hand, volunteer, and, best

Consonant digraphs:

> cheer, with, when, shield, chills, cheers

Plural **-s** as in **dogs/boxes/babies:**

> tunes, bands, stands, wings, clowns, ears, lions, eyes, rockets, chills, cheers, souvenirs

Short vowels:

> fun, bands, stands, an, acrobat, swings, as, with, wings, laugh, when, funny, hand, volunteer, and, rockets, love, chills, but, best, of

FOCUSING TALK

▪ Quote the poem's last couplet any time the circus topic arises. Introduce children to the figurative use of the word *circus* by referring to a poorly planned event you attended (*or* a chaotic period in the classroom!) as a "circus."

▪ Innovate on the poem's last couplet to tell children about another place you love to go where you can bring home souvenirs. Examples might be a sports event, the symphony, a concert, a play, or an exhibition.

ACTIVITY: SOUVENIRS

Invite children to bring in souvenirs from events they've attended. Help children tell about the event and the significance of the souvenir.

LISTEN! LISTEN! HEAR THAT SOUND?

Initial	Medial	Final	near
earring	appearance	dear	reindeer
eerie	cheering	ear	souvenir
	fierce	fear	tier
	sincerely	here	year

Circus Cheer

I hear fun tunes by circus bands.
    I see a horse rear near the stands.
I cheer an acrobat who swings
    as fearless as a bird with wings.

I laugh when funny clowns appear.
    I wave my hand to volunteer.
I hold my ears when lions roar
    and shield my eyes when rockets soar.

I love the circus—
chills and cheers,
but best of all are . . .
souvenirs!

Jeanne B. Hargett

ear/eer/ier

ear

A Weird Beard

by
Babs Bell Hajdusiewicz

eer

ier

ear

eer

ier

TARGETED SOUND

R-controlled vowel digraph **ear/eer/ier** as in **hear/deer/pier:**

weird, beard, cashier, appears, clearly, spear, eerie, fearsome, weary, steer, clear

FOCUSING TALK

▪ Use the words *clearly resembles, eerie, fearsome,* and *weary* at every opportunity.

▪ When appropriate, quote the poem's words to say, "That appears to be weird," or "I'm gonna steer clear!"

ACTIVITY: WEIRD BEARDS

Provide outlines of faces on heavy paper or cardboard. Have children use glue and cotton balls, steel wool pads, or crumpled tissue paper to attach beards to the faces.

LISTEN! LISTEN! HEAR THAT SOUND?

Initial	Medial	Final
ear	disappeared	career
Erie	dreary	frontier
	pierce	gear
	volunteers	headgear
		rear
		severe
		sphere
		tear
		we're

A Weird Beard

That cashier has a beard
    that appears to be weird.
        It clearly resembles a spear.

He looks pretty eerie
    and fearsome and weary.
        I'll pay . . . but I'm gonna steer clear!

Babs Bell Hajdusiewicz

R-Controlled Digraphs:

ear/eer/ier

our/owr

our

Sir Sour

by
Naomi Grady

owr

our

owr

our

owr

TARGETED SOUND

R-controlled vowel digraph **our/owr** as in **hour/power:**

> Sour, our, late-hour, mee-our, sauerkraut, floured, soured, devours, sourdough, sour-full

ADDITIONAL SOUNDS

Consonant **s**/soft **c** as in **so/city:**

> Sir Sour, sour, sauerkraut, soup, sardines, juice, soured, some, sour-dough, sour-full

Long vowels:

> likes, eat, foods, late-hour, treats, mee-our, he, soup, sardines, juice, goop, cries, beet, green, feet, cream, too, stew, sourdough, to

FOCUSING TALK

▪ Tease children by saying that lunch will consist of all sour foods, such as sour pickles, sauerkraut, sour milk, etc.

▪ Refer to someone as "Sir Sour" when the person is eating a sour food, such as sourdough bread or a lemon drop.

ACTIVITY: SOUR MILK

Provide a measuring cup, eyedropper or measuring spoons, milk, and vinegar. Help children make sweet milk turn to sour milk by adding drops of vinegar to a cup of milk.

LISTEN! LISTEN! HEAR THAT SOUND?

Initial	Medial	Final
hourly	coward	cower
our	Howard	flour
ours		flower
		power
		tower

Sir Sour

Our cat, Sir Sour,
likes to eat
sour foods for late-hour treats.

"Mee-our," he howls
for sauerkraut soup,
and sour sardines,
and sour juice goop.

"Mee-our," he cries
for a sour red beet
and sour green peppers
and floured pigs' feet.

He laps sour milk
and sour cream, too.
Then Sour slurp-slurps
soured halibut stew.

Sir Sour devours
some sourdough bread.
And sour-full, Sour
waddles off to his bed.

Naomi Grady

R-Controlled Digraphs:

our/owr

our/owr

our

Dinner Hour

by
Babs Bell Hajdusiewicz

owr

our

owr

our

owr

TARGETED SOUND

R-controlled vowel digraph **our/owr** as in **hour/power:**

hour, flowers, cower, devour, shower, power

FOCUSING TALK

▪ Innovate on the poem's words at lunchtime to compare hungry children to thirsty flowers. For example, you might say, "Children cower, then devour lunch food's power—lunchtime hour!"

▪ Refer to rain as "shower power." Substitute *devour* for *eat,* and use *cower* to describe someone who is hesitating or standing off to the side, perhaps out of shyness.

ACTIVITY: TOWERING FLOWERS

Provide pipe cleaners, paper and fabric scraps, tissue paper, and glue for children's use in creating tall-stemmed flowers. Children can cut out leaves and petals or make flowers out of crumpled tissue paper. Children may wish to "plant" the flowers in pots of soil or in clay.

LISTEN! LISTEN! HEAR THAT SOUND?

Initial	Medial	Final
hours	devoured	dour
ours	overpowered	glower
	sauerkraut	scour
	scoured	sour
	towered	

Dinner Hour

Flowers cower,
then devour
shower power—

Dinner hour!

Babs Bell Hajdusiewicz

R-Controlled Digraphs:

our/owr

Prefixes

dis- as in ***discover***

un- as in ***unable***

re- as in ***review***

Suffixes

-ful as in ***careful***

-less as in ***careless***

-ness as in ***kindness***

-ly as in ***lonely***

dis

dis

Disorder

by
Babs Bell Hajdusiewicz

dis

dis

dis

dis

dis

TARGETED SOUND

Prefix **dis-** as in **discover:**

> disorder, displeasing, distasteful, disruptive, disgraceful, disgusting, disown

> (Note that *dis-* precedes a root word in the following words: disruptive, disgusting.)

ADDITIONAL SOUNDS

Contractions:

> it's, I've

Long vowels:

> displeasing, distasteful, disgraceful, though, I've, grown, I, disown

FOCUSING TALK

▪ Quote the poem any time your desk or personal items are in disarray. Or innovate on the poem's words to say "you've" and "you" as you comment on someone else's apparent disorganization.

▪ Use the poem's *dis-* words when you are requesting children's cooperation. For example, to encourage children to tidy up, you might say, "This disorder is displeasing," or "Let's make this disorder disappear."

ACTIVITY: DISAPPEARING DISORDER

Scramble alphabet letter cards or magnetic letters and invite children to put them in order while singing the "ABC Song." At another time, lay out red, orange, yellow, green, blue, indigo, and violet crayons (in that order) to simulate the colors of the rainbow from outside to inside. Help children sing the color names, in proper order, to the tune of "Twinkle Twinkle."

LISTEN! LISTEN! HEAR THAT SOUND?

Initial
disadvantage
disagree
disappear
disappoint
disarm
disband
disprove

Disorder

It's displeasing.
It's distasteful.
It's disruptive.
It's disgraceful.

This disorder,
though I've grown it,
is disgusting!
I disown it!

Babs Bell Hajdusiewicz

dis

dis

A "Dis" Kind of Day?

by
Karen O'Donnell Taylor

dis

dis

dis

dis

TARGETED SOUND

Prefix **dis-** as in **discover:**

> disturbed, disgusted, disgruntled, disheartened, displeased, distrusted, disruptive, disliked, discounted, distress, dismay, dishonored, dismantled, disjointed

(Note that *dis-* precedes a root word in the following words: disturbed, disgusted, disgruntled, disruptive, distress, dismay.*)*

ADDITIONAL SOUNDS

Contractions:

> I'm, it's

Ending **-d/-ed** as in **hoped/waited:**

> disturbed, disgusted, disgruntled, disheartened, displeased, distrusted, disliked, discounted, dishonored, dismantled, disjointed

FOCUSING TALK

▪ Try using some of the poem's words to convey a message about an inappropriate behavior. For instance, you might say, "I'm feeling disturbed and disheartened. I'm full of distress and dismay." You might also use the poem's words to acknowledge a child who is feeling "left out" of an activity. In this case, you might say, "You're feeling displeased and discounted."

▪ Challenge children's listening skills by using words and their opposites in routine conversation. For example, you might say, "I liked-disliked that movie," "This is a thick-thin book," or "I trust-distrust your opinion." Encourage children to comment on your "strange" way of talking.

ACTIVITY: FACE UP, FACE DOWN

You will need two sets of magnetic alphabet letters for this activity. Depending on children's skill level, select several letters and their matches. Turn one set face up, and the other face down. Have children find each letter's match. Repeat the activity for other letters of the alphabet or for magnetic numbers.

LISTEN! LISTEN! HEAR THAT SOUND?

Initial

discharge	dishonest	disposal
discredit	dismount	dissatisfied

A "Dis" Kind of Day?

I'm feeling disturbed
    and disgusted
and somewhat disgruntled today.

I'm feeling disheartened,
    displeased,
      and distrusted,
and downright disruptive, I say!

I'm feeling disliked and discounted.
I'm full of distress and dismay.

I'm feeling dishonored,
    dismantled,
    disjointed—
Perhaps 'cause it's "opposites" day.

Karen O'Donnell Taylor

Prefixes and Suffixes:

dis

un

un

Me a Mess?

by
Babs Bell Hajdusiewicz

un

un un

un

un

TARGETED SOUND

Prefix **un-** as in **unable:**

> unclean, unbuckled, unfastened, untied, unfit, undignified, unfolded, unbuttoned, unbecoming, unfortunately, unaware

ADDITIONAL SOUNDS

Ending **-d/-ed** as in **hoped/waited:**

> unbuckled, unfastened, untied, undignified, unfolded, unbuttoned, unbecoming

Long vowel **e** as in **me:**

> me, unclean, be, seen, unbecoming

Short vowels:

> mess, and, unbuckled, unfastened, unfit, undignified, unbuttoned, less

FOCUSING TALK

- Model reading or reciting the poem while shaking your head "no" as you pronounce the "un" in each word. At another time, substitute the word *not* for the prefix *un.*

- Talk about *unclean* or *unfolded* laundry, *unbuttoned* or *untied* clothing, *unacceptable* behavior, an *uncomplicated* task, *undisturbed* sleep, or an *unbecoming* hairstyle or garment.

ACTIVITY: OPPOSITES

Encourage children to use fabric or paper scraps, paper clips, twist ties, string, rubberbands, old button-front shirts, and belts to demonstrate and talk about the use of opposite words such as *covered* and *uncovered, attached* and *unattached, tied* and *untied, opened* and *unopened, buttoned* and *unbuttoned, buckled* and *unbuckled, twisted* and *untwisted, stretched* and *unstretched,* or *fastened* and *unfastened.*

LISTEN! LISTEN! HEAR THAT SOUND?

Initial

unable	unhealthy
unbeaten	unheard of
uncomfortable	unlikely
unconcerned	unsure
undone	unusual

Me a Mess?

Unclean and unbuckled,
Unfastened, untied,
Unfit to be seen,
I'm undignified.
Unfolded, unbuttoned,
Unbecoming, no less.
Unfortunately, I'm
Unaware I'm a mess.

Babs Bell Hajdusiewicz

Prefixes and Suffixes:

un

un

un

Unlikely, It Seems

by
Carol Murray

TARGETED SOUND

Prefix **un-** as in **unable:**

unlikely, unhappy, unaware, unable, unearthly, unless, unreal

ADDITIONAL SOUNDS

Long vowel **e** as in **me:**

unlikely, seems, unhappy, Lee, knee, he, be, see, dreams, he's, screaming, squeal, Lee's, unreal

Suffix **-ly** as in **lonely:**

unlikely, unearthly, clearly

FOCUSING TALK

▪ Quote the poem's title whenever you're questioning the truth of something. If appropriate, you might go on to say that something is "clearly unreal" or that it's "never been born."

▪ Innovate on the poem's words to say, "Unaware must *I* be, quite unable to see . . . ," when you are feeling puzzled.

ACTIVITY: UNEARTHLY CREATURES

Have children illustrate some "unearthly creatures." For contrast, ask children to situate their creatures in habitats or surroundings that appear to be quite "earthly," such a cage in a zoo, a tree in a forest, a pet bed in a home, or a body of water.

LISTEN! LISTEN! HEAR THAT SOUND?

Initial
uncombed
uneaten
unequaled
unfamiliar
unintended
unloving
unmade
unnoticed
unofficial

Unlikely, It Seems

Unhappy is Lee,
with a bump on his knee—
from the thrust of a unicorn's horn.

Unaware must he be,
quite unable to see,
that a unicorn's never been born!

Unlikely, it seems,
since it's only in dreams.
But he's screaming an unearthly squeal.

Now
unless I'm mistaken,
Lee's story is fakin'—
a unicorn's clearly unreal.

Carol Murray

un

An Unfriendly Monster

by
Babs Bell Hajdusiewicz

TARGETED SOUND

Prefix **un-** as in **unable:**

> unfriendly, unusual, unpleasant, unruly, unbearably, uneasy, unbelievably

ADDITIONAL SOUNDS

Contractions:

> I'll, they'll

Suffix **-ly** as in **lonely:**

> unfriendly, unruly, unbearably, unbelievably

FOCUSING TALK

- Innovate on the poem's first line in lieu of saying "no" to a child's request: "I'd be in a strange and unusual mood if you were to do that."

- Innovate on the poem to describe a different Halloween character. For instance, you might describe a *friendly* monster with words such as "I'll be in a friendly, cooperative mood. I'll be acting with kindness. I *will* not be rude. I'll make an incredibly monster-ish sound, but they'll be delighted when I come around."

ACTIVITY: AN UNFRIENDLY MONSTER

Provide old magazines and catalogs. Have children cut out pictures of various body parts belonging to people and animals, along with pictures of tools, appliances, or other common household objects. Invite children to assemble cutouts to create unusually odd creatures. For example, a creature might have a refrigerator body, an animal's head, and tools for legs and arms.

LISTEN! LISTEN! HEAR THAT SOUND?

Initial

unable	unequal
unbeatable	unfair
uncovered	unhooked
undecided	untied
undo	

An Unfriendly Monster

I'll be in a strange and unusual mood.
I'll be acting unpleasant,
    unruly,
      and rude.
I'll make an unbearably
    monster-ish sound.
And *they'll* be uneasy
    when I come around.
I'll be unbelievably monstrous
    and mean
As an unfriendly monster—
    come next Halloween!

Babs Bell Hajdusiewicz

Prefixes and Suffixes:

un

re

re
Requirements

by
Heidi Roemer

TARGETED SOUND

Prefix **re-** as in **review:**

requirements, review, respond, reviewed, remain, recess, rewrite, released, relieved, remake, rehang, rethink, retire

(Note that *re-* precedes a root word in the following words: requirements, remain, recess, relieved, retired.)

ADDITIONAL SOUNDS

Contractions:

I've, I'm, it's, school's, I'll

Long vowel **i** as in **like:**

requirements, my, I, I've, I'm, rewrite, I'll, retired

FOCUSING TALK

▪ Draw on the poem to say, "I have a request," or "Do you have a request?" when asking questions or when responding to children's requests. Talk about how retirement may mean being through with certain requests and requirements, but that other demands take their place.

▪ Quote the poem to say, "So many requests and requirements to do!" when you or children seem to have too much to do.

ACTIVITY: BEFORE AND AFTER RETIREMENT

Invite children to interview a parent or an adult family friend. Have the child find out about one thing the person does now that he or she will no longer do during retirement and one thing the person does not do now that he or she will do during retirement. Have children divide a sheet of paper in half and draw or cut out pictures to illustrate the person's two responses. Ask children to use their pictures to tell about the interview.

LISTEN! LISTEN! HEAR THAT SOUND?

Initial

react	rediscover	repeat
rearrange	refill	replace
rebound	rename	reproduce
rebuilt	reopen	rewrap
recover		

Requirements

My teacher requests me to read and review.
I respond that I've done it—reviewed it.
I'm through.

My teacher requests I remain in my seat.
No recess until
I rewrite and it's neat.

At last, I'm released.
School's done for the day.
I pack up my things.
I'm relieved—I can play!

But Mom has requests:
I must remake my bed.
And rehang my clothes.
And rethink what I've said.

So many requests and requirements to do.
Someday I'll be old—
and retired—
and be . . . through?

Heidi Roemer

Prefixes and Suffixes:

re

re

re

Earth Says

by
Babs Bell Hajdusiewicz

TARGETED SOUND

Prefix **re-** as in **review:**

reduce, recycle, reuse, refuse

(Note that *re-* precedes a root word in the following words: reduce, refuse.)

ADDITIONAL SOUNDS

Long vowel **u** as in **pool:**

oodles, lose, choose

Long vowel **u** as in **view:**

cues, reduce, reuse, refuse, abuse

FOCUSING TALK

▪ You'll find the phrases "I'm giving you oodles of cues . . ." and "It's time to refuse . . ." can be helpful ways to introduce gentle reminders.

▪ Talk about the kinds of cues that the Earth gives us that tell us we need to recycle and conserve our resources.

ACTIVITY: RECYCLED NOTE PADS

Collect used sheets of paper that have one clean side. Help children use a paper cutter to cut the sheets in halves or in fourths. Similarly, cut old tablet (cardboard) backs in halves or fourths. Stack several pieces of paper on a cardboard back and staple together or "bind" with yarn to make a note pad. To personalize the pads, especially if giving as a gift to a loved one, children might wish to decorate them or add a fingerprint to a corner of each page.

LISTEN! LISTEN! HEAR THAT SOUND?

Initial
recall
recite
recoil
recollect
reconsider
reissue
remind
replace
return

Earth Says

I'm giving you oodles of cues
To reduce, recycle, reuse.
It's time to refuse
The choice to abuse
Or lose your freedom to choose.

Babs Bell Hajdusiewicz

Prefixes and Suffixes:

re

ful

ful

Handfuls of Thanks

by
Sydnie Meltzer Kleinhenz

TARGETED SOUND

Suffix **-ful** as in **careful:**

handfuls, skillful, careful, playful, graceful, wonderful, helpful, thankful

ADDITIONAL SOUNDS

Contraction:

we're

Long vowels:

we, tie, bows, clothes, write, name, playful, video, game, graceful, any

Short vowels:

handfuls, of, thanks, with, thumbs, skillful, when, snap, up, video, knob, wonderful, at, job, glad, have, helpful, chums, fingers, thankful, thumbs

FOCUSING TALK

▪ Innovate on the poem's text to compliment children's successes. For instance, you might say, "You're careful when you write your name," or "You're playful with a video game."

▪ Quote lines from the poem as if your thumbs are speaking. Or substitute *we're* for *they're* to comment on a child's thumbs.

ACTIVITY: PLAYFUL THUMB BALL

Provide a tiny rubber ball or Ping-Pong ball, along with cardboard tubes from tissue paper or paper toweling. Using only the thumbs, the first player must place the ball inside a tube and pass the ball to a second player's tube. That player passes it to the third player, and so on. Play stops and begins anew when a player drops the ball. Players attempt to pass the ball from player to player until the last player's tube contains the ball.

LISTEN! LISTEN! HEAR THAT SOUND?

Medial	Final
cheerfully	awful
gratefully	hateful
helpfulness	mindful
playfully	playful
skillfully	plentiful
	powerful

Handfuls of Thanks

With thumbs for partners,
   we tie bows.
We're skillful
   when we snap up clothes.
We're careful
   when we write a name.
We're playful
   with a video game.
We're graceful
   when we turn a knob.
We're wonderful
   at any job.
We're glad we have
   our helpful chums.
We're fingers—
   thankful for our thumbs.

Sydnie Meltzer Kleinhenz

Prefixes and Suffixes:

ful

ful

ful

Joyful Finish

by
Babs Bell Hajdusiewicz

ful

ful *ful*

ful

ful

ful

TARGETED SOUND

Suffix **-ful** as in **careful:**

> joyful, doubtful, fearful, tearful, painful, fretful, fateful, grateful, helpful, cheerful

ADDITIONAL SOUNDS

Long vowels:

> even, feeling, be, painful, I, might, die, fateful, grateful, coach, me, to, try

FOCUSING TALK

■ Innovate on the poem's words to acknowledge a child's satisfaction in accomplishing a task. For example, you might say, "You were doubtful. You were fearful. . . ." You'll want to encourage children to edit the words as needed to reflect their exact feelings—that is, a child might say, "I wasn't really fearful."

■ Tell children about a time when you experienced a joyful finish. Begin by telling them about the task you were attempting. Then quote the poem or innovate on its words to express how you were feeling before, during, and after the activity.

ACTIVITY: HELPFUL COACHING

Have children work in pairs, with one child performing a task and the other acting as "coach" offering encouragement. Have each pair set a goal—say, a physical activity, such as jumping jacks or push-ups, or a challenging writing or reading task. Help the "coach" use positive words of encouragement, and help the "doer" recite the poem to announce a "joyful finish."

LISTEN! LISTEN! HEAR THAT SOUND?

Medial	Final
awfully	beautiful
hatefulness	distasteful
hopefulness	fearful
joyfully	forgetful
thankfully	hopeful

Joyful Finish

I was doubtful.
I was fearful.
I was even feeling tearful.
I was scared that it'd be painful.
I was fretful I might die!

But I did it!
(t'wasn't fateful!)
I am joyful!
I am grateful
that my helpful coach was cheerful
and encouraged me to try.

Babs Bell Hajdusiewicz

ful

ful

Tearful Night Noises

by
Lois Muehl

ful

ful

ful

ful

ful

ful

TARGETED SOUND

Suffix **-ful** as in **careful:**

tearful, cheerful, earful, fearful

ADDITIONAL SOUNDS

Long vowel **i** as in **like:**

I, my, cries, night, like, sight

R-controlled vowel digraph **ear/eer** as in **hear/deer:**

tearful, cheerful, earful, fearful

FOCUSING TALK

▪ Innovate on the poem's words to gently remind children to work or play carefully. For example, you might say, "I am hopeful this will be done carefully."

▪ Quote lines from the poem, such as "I am never very cheerful . . ." or "like magic, he turns cheerful," to gently remind children of a rule or to comment on a child's reaction to a surprise.

ACTIVITY: TEARFUL NIGHT NOISES

Ask children to draw or cut out pictures that illustrate noises that would frighten them at night. Display the pictures or collect them in a book titled *Tearful Night Noises.*

LISTEN! LISTEN! HEAR THAT SOUND?

Medial	Final
carefully	awful
cheerfulness	doubtful
doubtfully	grateful
helpfulness	hopeful
thoughtfully	mindful
	wonderful

Tearful Night Noises

I am never very cheerful
    when I have to get an earful
        of my baby brother's tearful cries at night.

When he cries out, I am fearful,
    though, like magic, he turns cheerful
        when our mama and his bottle are in sight.

Lois Muehl

Prefixes and Suffixes:

ful

less

less

Supperless Mouse

by
Jean Parker Katz

less

less

less

less

less

TARGETED SOUND

Suffix **-less** as in **careless:**

> supperless, noiseless, harmlessly, tasteless, heartless, voiceless, lifeless, mouseless

ADDITIONAL SOUNDS

Diphthong **ou/ow** as in **out/cow:**

> mouse, mouseless, house

Long vowels:

> feet, to, eat, he, spied, cheese, sighed, I'd, be, lifeless, leave

Short vowels:

> supperless, on went, something, some, in, trap, with set, snap, and that, crept, bed

FOCUSING TALK

▪ Call upon the poem's words and ideas to gently remind children of your expectations: "Let's use our noiseless feet and voiceless jaws to create a noiseless room," or "Let's move down the hall on noiseless feet."

▪ Talk about a time when you went harmlessly looking for food or a time when you went to bed supperless because of illness, lack of a food you wanted, or simple loss of appetite.

ACTIVITY: PAPERLESS WRITING

Have children work in pairs and use index fingers to "write" numbers or letters in the air for partners to identify. Children might also draw simple pictures, such as a heart, smiley face, or circle, in the air for partners to identify.

LISTEN! LISTEN! HEAR THAT SOUND?

Medial	Final	
carelessly	ageless	shirtless
carelessness	careless	shoeless
fearlessly	cordless	thoughtless
hopelessness	keyless	tireless
	mindless	

Supperless Mouse

A supperless mouse
    on noiseless feet
    went harmlessly searching
    for something to eat.

He spied some cheese
    in a heartless trap
    with voiceless jaws
    all set to snap.

Mouse sighed, "I'd be
    a lifeless mouse
    and that would
    leave a mouseless house!"

A supperless mouse
    on noiseless feet
    crept off to bed
    with nothing to eat.

Jean Parker Katz

Prefixes and Suffixes:

less

less

Blast Off!

by
Joanne Oppenheim

less

less

less

less

TARGETED SOUND

Suffix **-less** as in **careless:**

wheelless, wingless, weightless

ADDITIONAL SOUND

Consonant **w** as in **wet:**

wingless, weightless, await

FOCUSING TALK

▪ Compare the poem's idea of "unknowns" in space to the idea that the future is unknown. When introducing children to a new book or new facts in math or science, for example, you might say, "Unknown roads of joy await us," or you might substitute specific words in the sentence, such as "words to read," "science facts," or "number facts" in the sentence.

▪ Describe a running child, a leaf blowing in the wind, a child on a swing, or a piece of dust in the air as "wheelless and wingless." In addition, you might describe yourself as "penless" or "paperless" when you can't find writing tools you need. Children will be interested in comparing the sounds and spellings of the homophones *waitless* and *weightless.*

ACTIVITY: WEIGHTLESS AND WAITLESS

Have children draw a line to divide a sheet of paper in half. Ask children to illustrate *weightless* and *waitless.* Ideas for *weightless* might include astronauts in space or an empty scale; those for *waitless* as being first in line to get tickets for a movie or an amusement park ride, or getting picked up by a bus or parent at school.

LISTEN! LISTEN! HEAR THAT SOUND?

Medial	Final
helplessly	clueless
helplessness	fearless
hopelessly	fruitless
tirelessness	headless
	helpless
	joyless
	motionless
	ticketless
	wireless

Blast Off!

Wheelless
wingless
weightless

unknown roads in space await us.

Joanne Oppenheim

ness

ness

Togetherness

by
Dee Lillegard

ness

ness

ness

ness

ness

TARGETED SOUND

Suffix **-ness** as in **kindness:**

> togetherness, silliness, filthiness, stubbornness, kindness, goodness, cleanliness, neatness, brightness

ADDITIONAL SOUNDS

Blends:

> think, fly, and, stubbornness, kindness, wings, cleanliness, things, went, brought, brightness

Consonant digraphs:

> togetherness, think, that, this, there, filthiness, with, wash, wretched, things, washed, they're

Long vowels:

> togetherness, you, may, silliness, fly, so, filthiness, oh, my, lady, kindness, cleanliness, neatness, to, time, by, brightness, life, away, wife

FOCUSING TALK

■ Children will enjoy your playfulness when you introduce a conversation by quoting the poem's first line. Similarly, quote the poem to say, "My goodness, wash your wings!" when a child is about to wash up.

■ Innovate on the poem's line, "He washed away his stubbornness," to comment that a child has "washed away" errors on a paper, "washed away" a frown, "washed away" a conflict, or the like. Similarly, show appreciation for a child's cheerfulness by saying, "You've brought brightness to our lives."

ACTIVITY: BRIGHTNESS IN MY LIFE

Ask children to draw or cut out pictures that illustrate joy in their lives. Children might draw spotlights all around their pictures or add a sun or full moon.

LISTEN! LISTEN! HEAR THAT SOUND?

Final

carelessness	hopelessness
darkness	lateness
helpfulness	messiness
helplessness	sweetness

Togetherness

You may think that this is silliness,
but once there was a fly,
a fly so full of filthiness
and stubbornness—oh, my!

A lady fly, with kindness,
said, "My goodness, wash your wings!"
But cleanliness and neatness,
to that fly, were wretched things.

As time went by, the lady fly
brought brightness to his life.
He washed away his stubbornness,
and now they're Fly and Wife.

Dee Lillegard

Prefixes and Suffixes:

ness

ness

ness

Introduction

by
William Cole

ness

ness

ness

ness

TARGETED SOUND

Suffix **-ness** as in **kindness:**

silliness, willy-nilliness, hillybilliness, hilliness, craziness, dayziness, gayziness, horseplayziness, sapiness, slaphappiness, cappiness, lappiness, ghostliness, ghoulishness, poolishness, schoolishness, foolishness.

ADDITIONAL SOUNDS

Short vowel **i** as in **pin:**

introduction, silliness, silly, willy-nilliness, hillybilliness, hilliness, April, giddy, ridiculous, his, into, hilarity, stairity, tipping, chairity, hairity, ghoulishness, him, in, poolishness, schoolishness, foolishness

Consonant **y** as **e** as in **very:**

silly, willy, willy-nilliness, dopey, hillybilliness, giddy, goopy, bumpy, hilarity, stairity, chairity, hairity

FOCUSING TALK

▪ Children will enjoy hearing you use the poem's coined words during conversations. For example, refer to children's playfulness as "horseplayziness" or "slaphappiness," or comment on a lazy kind of day as "lazy-dayziness" or a time of silliness as "foolish-schoolishness."

▪ You'll want to quote individual stanzas or the entire poem when you or children are having fun with silliness.

ACTIVITY: OH, SUCH SILLINESS!

Have children illustrate silly things they've seen or thought about. Children will enjoy dictating words that tell about their pictures or simply using the poem's words as captions. Compile the pictures in a book titled "Oh, Such Silliness!"

LISTEN! LISTEN! HEAR THAT SOUND?

Final
goodness
happiness
joyfulness
kindliness
openness
sadness
willfulness

Introduction

Oh, such silliness!
Silly willy-nilliness,
Dopey hillybilliness,
Rolling down the hilliness!

Oh, such craziness!
First of April Dayziness,
Giddy, goopy gayziness,
Bumpy dumb horseplayziness!

Oh, such sappiness!
Ridiculous slaphappiness,
Throw away his cappiness,
Jump into his lappiness!

Oh, such hilarity!
Falling down the stairity,
Tipping over chairity,
Shaving off your hairity!

Ghostliness and ghoulishness!
Push him in the poolishness,
Staying home from schoolishness—
Oh, such foolishness!

William Cole

Prefixes and Suffixes:

ness

ly

ly

Tortoise and Hare

(or: Slow, Slow, Quick, Quick, Slow . . .)

by
Judith Nicholls

TARGETED SOUND

Suffix **-ly** as in **lonely:**

slowly, calmly, quickly, swiftly, briefly, proudly

ADDITIONAL SOUNDS

Blend **st** as in **stop:**

stared, stepped, starting, past, stopped, rest

R-blends:

crawled, track, through, prize, briefly, proudly, dreams

FOCUSING TALK

▪ Call upon the following lines to comment on children's actions: "Slowly stepped towards the line and waited there," "briefly stopped to take a rest," "sped swiftly for the prize." Similarly, you might innovate on the poem's words to say, "Quickly, the child ran out of sight," or ". . . calmly watched the clock tick on."

▪ Refer to children as "tortoises" when they complete tasks or when they methodically plan before they act.

ACTIVITY: POSITIVELY MINE

Have children draw or cut out pictures of things they own. Examples might include a favorite stuffed animal or blanket, clothing items, facial features, toys, a bedroom at home, a bicycle, books, etc. Encourage children to collect their pictures and add a personal photograph to make a book titled "Positively Mine."

LISTEN! LISTEN! HEAR THAT SOUND?

Final

absolutely	positively
beautifully	powerfully
dearly	similarly
frequently	sincerely
hopefully	suddenly
lovely	wonderfully

Tortoise and Hare

(or: Slow, Slow, Quick, Quick, Slow . . .)

Slowly the tortoise raised her head,
stared slowly at the hare;
slowly stepped towards the line
and waited there.

Calmly she heard the starting gun,
crawled calmly down the track;
calmly watched the hare race on
and not look back.

Quickly the hare ran out of sight,
chased quickly through the wood;
quickly fled through fern and moss,
through leaf and mud.

Swiftly he leapt past hedge and field,
sped swiftly for his prize;
briefly stopped to take a rest—
and closed his eyes.

Slowly the tortoise reached the wood,
slowly she ambled on.
The hare raced proudly through his dreams;
the tortoise won.

Judith Nicholls

Prefixes and Suffixes:

ly

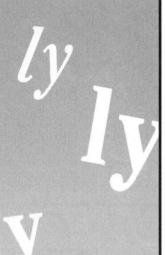

ly

ly
Totally Messy Milk

by
Susan D. Anderson

TARGETED SOUND

Suffix **-ly** as in **lonely:**

> totally, intently, gently, slowly, freely, carefully, calmly, quickly, hopefully

ADDITIONAL SOUNDS

Short vowels:

> messy, milk, intently, gently, spills, on, quickly, mop, Mom, top

FOCUSING TALK

■ Quote the first three lines of the poem as you carefully pour a liquid. Of course, you'll want to continue to the poem's fourth line, should you accidentally spill the liquid! Similarly, quote the appropriate lines from the poem when you or a child is cleaning up a spill.

■ Innovate on the poem's last line when you're hoping that someone will not be upset.

ACTIVITY: POURING AND CLEANING

Provide a liquid, several containers, and a sponge for children to use in practicing pouring and then cleaning up spilled drops. Encourage children to innovate on the poem as appropriate to talk about their actions while pouring and cleaning.

LISTEN! LISTEN! HEAR THAT SOUND?

Final
awfully
calmly
certainly
gratefully
kindly
openly
partially
proudly
rapidly
socially
surely
truly

Totally Messy Milk

Intently,
    Gently,
        Slowly pour—
Milk spills freely on the floor.

Carefully,
    Calmly,
        Quickly mop—

Hopefully, Mom won't blow her top.

Susan D. Anderson

Prefixes and Suffixes:

ly

Contractions

'm as in *I'm*

'd as in *you'd*

'll as in *I'll*

're as in *you're*

Silent Letters

gh as in *sigh*

w as in *write*

k as in *knit*

b as in *doubt*

c as in *sick*

'm

Playing I'm King

by
Katherine Burton

TARGETED SOUND

Contraction:

I'm

ADDITIONAL SOUNDS

L-blends:

playing, slurping, play, climbing

Blends:

king, jumping, twirling, spinning, around, swinging, swaying, ground

Consonant digraphs:

munching, shouting, whirling, touching

Ending **-ing** as in **going:**

playing, slurping, munching, laughing, jumping, shouting, whirling, twirling, spinning, swinging, swaying, touching, running, climbing, feeling

 FOCUSING TALK

■ Quote any of the poem's stanzas, as appropriate, to reflect your own or children's feelings or actions.

■ Refer to yourself or a child as "King" or "Queen" of the "hill." At times, customize the words by changing *hill* to *class, game, room, playground,* or *day.*

 ACTIVITY: I'M WISHING . . .

Invite each child to illustrate a wish. Display the illustrations under the caption "I'm Wishing . . . ."

 LISTEN! LISTEN! HEAR THAT SOUND?

Final

aren't	we've
can't	weren't
couldn't	where's
hasn't	wouldn't
he's	you've
I'd	

Playing I'm King

I'm slurping,
I'm munching,
I'm ready to play.

I'm laughing,
I'm jumping,
I'm shouting, "Hooray!"

I'm whirling,
I'm twirling,
I'm spinning around.

I'm swinging,
I'm swaying,
I'm touching the ground.

I'm running,
I'm climbing,
I'm King of the hill!

I'm King . . . but I'm feeling . . . I'm gonna be ill.

Katherine Burton

Contractions:

'm

'm

I'm Your Friend

by
Carol Murray

'd, m

're

'll

'd

TARGETED SOUND

Contractions:

I'm, you'd, I'll, you're

ADDITIONAL SOUNDS

Long vowel **o** as in **rope:**

go, hoping, know

Short vowels:

friend, happy, sad, when, wishing, and, that, ready

FOCUSING TALK

▪ You'll want to quote individual lines from the poem, or innovate on the words as needed, frequently to encourage children that you are nearby to offer help and support. Similarly, innovate on the poem's words to recognize a child's feelings when he or she is leaving others or is being left behind by others.

▪ Use the contractions *I'm* and *you're* as you express your feelings about a child's cooperative *or* uncooperative behavior.

ACTIVITY: I'M SMILING . . .

Provide old magazines for children's use in cutting out pictures of smiling mouths. Ask children to begin a sentence with "I'm smiling because . . ." to tell classmates why each mouth is smiling.

LISTEN! LISTEN! HEAR THAT SOUND?

Final

don't
he'd
here's
I've
it's
mustn't
that'd
they'd
they've
what's
who's

I'm Your Friend

I'm happy to see you.
I'm sad when you go.
I'm wishing you'd stay
    and
I'm hoping you know
    that
I'll be around
and ready to play.
I'm always your friend
even when you're away.

Carol Murray

gh/k

gh

A Mighty Knight

by
Babs Bell Hajdusiewicz

k

gh

k

gh

k

TARGETED SOUND

Silent letters **gh/k** as in **sigh/knight:** mighty, knight, fights, sunlight, nighttime, flashlight, midnight, frightened, nighty-night, nightlight

ADDITIONAL SOUNDS

Consonant **n** as in **not:** knight, in, sunlight, nighttime, midnight, frightened, nighty-night

Consonant **t** as in **top:** mighty, knight, daytime, fights, sunlight, at, nighttime, flashlight, but, midnight, frightened, nighty-night, nightlight

Long vowel **i** as in **like:** mighty, knight, daytime, fights, sunlight, nighttime, by, flashlight, midnight, frightened, nighty-night, nightlight

FOCUSING TALK

■ Children will enjoy hearing you substitute your name or a friend's in place of "a mighty knight."

■ Use the poem's division into three consecutive times of the day (daytime, nighttime, midnight) to present another idea. For example, you might tell children about being tired one morning and promising yourself you would go to bed earlier that night, only to find yourself busy at nighttime and *still* not ready for bed at midnight. Or, tell about planning to do a chore early in the day, but procrastinating all day long such that the chore is still undone at midnight.

ACTIVITY: A MIGHTY KNIGHT'S LIGHTS

Have children fold a sheet of paper in thirds. Help children draw or cut out pictures that depict the light sources (in order) for the three different times of day mentioned in the poem.

LISTEN! YOU *DON'T* HEAR THAT SOUND!

Medial		Final
bought	right	dough
bright	sight	high
brought	sought	sleigh
caught	straight	thigh
eight	thought	though
enough	weight	through
height		weigh

A Mighty Knight

In the daytime,
   a mighty knight
   fights mighty fights in the sunlight.
At nighttime,
   the mighty knight
   fights mighty fights by flashlight.
But at midnight,
   a mighty frightened knight
   goes nighty-night with a nightlight.

Babs Bell Hajdusiewicz

gh/w/k/b/c

gh

Fix It!
Quick!

by
Babs Bell Hajdusiewicz

w

k

b

c

gh

TARGETED SOUND

Silent letters **gh/w/k/b/c** as in **sigh, write, knit, doubt, sick:**

bought, night, right, though, write, quickly, typewriter's, sickly, know, doubt

ADDITIONAL SOUNDS

Consonant **t** as in **top:**

it, bought, night, but, doesn't, right, out, write, typewriter's, to, doubt

Long vowels:

I, night, right, leaves, silent, though, write, typewriter's, to, you'll, know, to, no

FOCUSING TALK

▪ Quote the poem's first two lines, or innovate on the words as needed, to tell children about something you purchased but had to return because it didn't work properly. Similarly, quote the poem's last line as you return a paper to a child who needs to make some corrections.

▪ Say, "I write with this quickly and it's working—*not* sickly," as you type on a typewriter or computer keyboard, or as you're writing with a pen.

ACTIVITY: WHAT'S MISSING?

Invite children to draw pictures that omit one or more important details. For example, children might draw a house with no windows, a face missing a facial feature, or a door with no doorknob. Have children identify missing details in friends' pictures.

LISTEN! YOU *DON'T* HEAR THAT SOUND!

Initial		Medial	Final
ghost	known	knight	back
gnaw	wrap	might	crumb
knapsack	wrestle	slight	climb
knee	wrist	tight	dumb
knife	wrong	unknown	high
knight	wrote	unwrap	slick
knob		unwritten	thumb

Fix It! QuiCk!

I bou**gh**t this last ni**gh**t,
But it doesn't work ri**gh**t.
It leaves silent consonants out!
Thou**gh** I **W**rite with it qui**C**kly,
This type**W**riter's si**C**kly.
You'll now **K**how to fix it, no dou**b**t!

Babs Bell Hajdusiewicz

Blackline Masters

Indexes

Acknowledgments

ch	wh	-ng
sh	-ft	-nk
th	-mp	-nt
	-nd	scr

More Phonics Through Poetry

shr	**str**	**ou/ow**
spl	**thr**	**-d/-ed**
spr	**au/aw**	**-er**
squ	**oi/oy**	**-est**

-ing	oo	y
-le	Schwa a	
a	Schwa e	-s/-es/ -ies
u	Schwa o	's

More Phonics Through Poetry

ar	**ear/ eer/ ier**	**re-**
or	**our/ owr**	**-ful**
ur	**dis-**	**-less**
air	**un-**	

-ness	'll	
-ly	're	
'm		
'd		

More Phonics Through Poetry

gh	b	
k	c	
w		
k		

Index

Title Index

Author Index

Index by First Line

Sound Index

Page numbers in bold type indicate poems in which the sound is heard with greatest frequency.

Blends

Final blends

-ft as in *left*, **41**, **43**, 45

-mp as in *lamp*, **47**, **49**

-nd as in *and*, **51**, **53**, 115, 117

-ng as in *sing*, **55**, **57**, 179

-nk as in *pink*, 27, **59**, **61**, **63**, 167

-nt as in *ant*, **65**, **67**, **69**

Various final blends, 45, 47, 125, 135, 139, 141, 159, 203, 205, 239, 249

Initial blends

L-Blends, 125, 139, 141, 165, 171, 173, 203, 205, 239, 249

R-Blends, 69, 107, 139, 158, 165, 173, 203, 205, 239, 243, 249

S-Blends

sc/sk as in *scare/sky*, 59

st as in *stop*, 243

Various *s*-blends, 61, 125, 139, 141, 165, 171, 173, 179, 203, 205, 239, 249

Various initial blends, 45, 47, 125, 133, 135, 139, 141, 159, 171, 173, 203, 205, 239, 249

3-letter blends

scr as in *scrap*, **73**, **75**

shr as in *shrub*, **77**, **79**

spl as in *splash*, **81**, **83**

spr as in *sprig*, **85**, **87**

str as in *string*, **93**, **95**, **97**

squ as in *squash*, **89**, **91**, 199

thr as in *three*, **99**, **101**

Various 3-letter blends, 47, 139, 165

Consonants

b as in *boy*, 143, 149, 153

d as in *dad*, 121, 143, 153, 189, 199

g as in *go*, 143, 193

h as in *he*, 51

j/soft *g* as in *joy/giant*, **67**

k/hard *c* as in *kite/cat*, 79, 105, 157

l as in *long*, 35, 41, 105, 111, 113, 127, 131, 149, 151

m as in *me*, 97

n as in *not*, 253

p as in *pet*, 57, 63

qu as in *quit*, 91

s/soft *c* as in *so/city*, 133, 195, 209

t as in *top*, 25, 155, 197, 199, 253, 255

w as in *wet*, 237

y as *e* as in *very* (see Vowels, Other Vowels)

y as *i* as in *sky* (see Vowels, Other Vowels)

Consonant Digraphs

ch as in *chin*, **15**, **17**,

sh as in *ship*, **19**, **21**, **23**, 83, 139, 159

th as in *thank*, **25**, **27**, **29**, 33

th as in *this*, 25, **31**, 33

wh as in *why*, **35**, **37**

Various consonant digraphs, 21, 133, 141, 171, 203, 205, 239, 249

Contractions, 97, 131, 145, 155, 161, 183, 215, 217, 223, 225, 229, **249**, **251**

Diphthongs

aw/aw as in *haul/claw*, **105**, **107** (see also Other Vowels *a* as in *ball/ought/claw*)

oi/oy as in *oil/boy*, **109**, **111**

ou/ow as in *out/cow*, 53, **113**, **115**, **117**, 163, 235

Endings

-d/-ed as in *hoped/waited*, 19, 43, 45, 47, 83, 107, **121**, **123**, 153, 217, 219

Theme Index

Acknowledgements

Unless otherwise noted, all poems by Babs Bell Hajdusiewicz are copyright © 1999 by the poet and Reprinted by permission.

"Index" from *The Idea Book* by Babs Bell Hajdusiewicz. Copyright © 1990 by MCP, Simon & Schuster Education Group. Reprinted by permission.

"Charlie's Chickens," "The Thinker," "I Did It!", and "A Mighty Knight" by Babs Bell Hajdusiewicz. Copyright © 1996 Babs Bell Hajdusiewicz. Published in *Don't Go Out in Your Underwear* by Dominie Press. Reprinted by permission of the author.

"The Search" by Heather Osborne. Copyright © 1999 by Heather Osborne. Reprinted by permission of the author.

"Posing" by Adelaide B. Shaw. Copyright © 1998 by Adelaide B. Shaw. Reprinted by permission of the author.

"Sheepshape" from *Ghastlies, Goops & Pincushions:* by X. J. Kennedy. Copyright © 1989 by X. J. Kennedy. Reprinted by permission of Margaret K. McElderry Books, an imprint of Simon & Schuster Children's Publishing Division and Curtis Brown, Ltd.

"Ocean Magic," "The Littlest Fish," and "Shrimply Delightful" by Bonnie Kerr Morris. Copyright © 1998 by Bonnie Kerr Morris. Reprinted by permission of the author.

"Toothpaste" by Stan Lee Werlin from *Highlights for Children*. Copyright © 1995 by Highlights for Children Inc., Columbus, Ohio, Reprinted by permission.

"Doublethink" from *Bing Bang Boing* by Douglas Florian. Copyright © 1994 by Douglas Florian. Reprinted by permission of Harcourt Brace & Company.

"Brother" from *Hello and Good-By* by Mary Ann Hoberman. Copyright © 1959, renewed 1987 by Mary Ann Hoberman. Reprinted by permission of Gina Maccoby Literary Agency.

"Whirly Wheels," "Playing I'm King," "Thirty Dirty Turtles," and "Twenty-four Things That I Like Best (And two that I don't)" by Katherine Burton. Copyright © 1998 by Katherine Burton. Reprinted by permission of the author.

"A Lift," "His Foibles," "Strutting with the Banjo Band," and "Togetherness" by Dee Lillegard. Copyright © 1998 by Dee Lillegard. Reprinted by permission of the author.

"Fifty Nifty Soldiers," "The Champ," and "Requirements" by Heidi Roemer. Copyright © 1998 by Heidi Roemer. Reprinted by permission of the author.

"Lumps" from *Flashlight and Other Poems* by Judith Thurman. Copyright © 1976 by Judith Thurman. Reprinted by permission of Marian Reiner for the author.

"Yolanda the Panda," "In Springtime," "Old Stravinsky," "A Quicker, Slicker Ride," "Bears," "Shouldn't, Couldn't, Wouldn't," "Unlikely It Seems," and "I'm Your Friend" by Carol Murray. Copyright © 1998 by Carol Murray. Reprinted by permission of the author.

"A Carelessly Crafted Raft," "An Astounding Legend," "Skink and Skunk," and "Whose Shoes" by Lucinda Cave. Copyright © 1997 by Lucinda Cave. Reprinted by permission of the author.

"Ode to Spring" from *The Collected Poems of Freddy the Pig* by Walter R. Brooks. Copyright © 1953 by Walter R. Brooks. Copyright renewed © 1981 by Dorothy R. Brooks. Reprinted by permission of Brandt & Brandt Literary Agents, Inc.

"Chipmunkskunkdonkmonkey" and "Scowling Owl" by Richard Michelson. Copyright © 1998 by Richard Michelson. Reprinted by permission of the author.

"Hummingbird" by Evelyn Amuedo Wade. Copyright © 1998 by Evelyn Amuedo Wade. Reprinted by permission of the author.

"Auntie's Elephant" and "Who's First" by Carol A. Losi. Copyright © 1998 by Carol A. Losi. Reprinted by permission of the author.

"Too Blunt" and "Conversations" by Ellen Raieta. Copyright © 1997 by Ellen Raieta. Reprinted by permission of the author.

"Scroungers," "Awesome Augie Auk," "Bulldog Bully," "Hardy Har Har," "Bird Alert," "Airfare," and "Fix It! Quick!" by Babs Bell Hajdusiewicz. Copyright © 1993 by Babs Bell Hajdusiewicz. Published in *Celebrate Reading!* by Scott Foresman. Reprinted by permission of the author.

"Under the Ground" by Babs Bell Hajdusiewicz. Copyright © 1991 by Babs Bell Hajdusiewicz. Previously published as "Subway" in *Poetry Works! The First Verse*. Copyright © 1993 by Modern Curriculum Press. Reprinted by permission of the author.

"Splish Splash Rain" by Marcia Swerdlow. Copyright © 1998 by Marcia Swerdlow. Reprinted by permission of the author.

"Quarrelsome Squirrels" by Karyn Mazo. Copyright © 1997 by Karyn Mazo. Reprinted by permission of the author.

"Striped Straps" by Bonnie Compton Hanson. Copyright © 1998 by Bonnie Compton Hanson. Reprinted by permission of the author.